Praise for *Stephen Ward Was Innocent, OK*

'There has been considerable disquiet about the prosecution
and conviction of Stephen Ward for half a century. But this
is the first time that the critical flaw in the proceedings – the
perjury of Christine Keeler – and its impact on the safety of
Ward's conviction have been set out with the utter clarity that
Geoffrey Robertson's considerable powers of legal analysis
bring. Robertson exposes what he describes as an "injustice
within the law". He sets out a compelling case, with proposed
grounds of appeal. This is a must-read for all those concerned
to understand how miscarriages of justice can arise.'
Keir Starmer QC, former Director of Public Prosecutions

'Geoffrey Robertson floods a dark corner of legal history with
brilliant light, exposing the lengths to which the Establishment
would go to protect the old order and to cover for their own.
A stunning exposé.'
Helena Kennedy QC

'Stephen Ward was a scapegoat and a victim both of calumny and a miscarriage of justice, which together drove him to suicide. In this compelling account, beautifully written and argued, Robertson rescues Ward's reputation from the lies and legal distortions that condemned him.'

A. C. Grayling

'A wonderfully clear dissection of a very grim period in British criminal justice. A thriller with a dark ending.'

Ken Macdonald QC

STEPHEN WARD WAS INNOCENT, OK

THE CASE FOR OVERTURNING HIS CONVICTION

GEOFFREY ROBERTSON

Biteback Publishing

In memory of John Mortimer

First published in Great Britain in 2013 by
Biteback Publishing Ltd
Westminster Tower
3 Albert Embankment
London SE1 7SP
Copyright © Geoffrey Robertson 2013

Page 1 top right, bottom; 2 top right, bottom; 3; 4; 5 top; 6; 7 © Press Association
Page 1 top left; 5 middle © Popperfoto/Getty Images; 5 bottom; 8 © Getty Images
Page 2 top left © reserved; collection National Portrait Gallery, London

Every reasonable effort has been made to trace copyright holders of material
reproduced in this book, but if any have been inadvertently overlooked the
publishers would be glad to hear from them.

ISBN 978-1-84954-690-4

10 9 8 7 6 5 4 3 2 1

A CIP catalogue record for this book is available from the British Library.

Set in Sabon and Franchise

Printed and bound in Great Britain by
CPI Group (UK) Ltd, Croydon CR0 4YY

MIX
Paper from
responsible sources
FSC
www.fsc.org
FSC® C020471

CONTENTS

PREFACE

The funeral of Stephen Ward, at Mortlake Cemetery in August 1963, attracted only six mourners – and they included his brothers and his solicitor. This distinguished osteopath and skilled portrait artist, a favourite of London's fashionable society throughout the 1950s, had died by his own hand. At the grave lay a wreath, made up of one hundred white carnations, and a card signed by Kenneth Tynan. It bore the simple inscription

To Stephen Ward,
Victim of Hypocrisy

That was true enough. Ward was put on trial at a time of moral panic, when the Christian complacency that had settled over British society after the war had been severely shaken by 'the Profumo affair'. John Profumo,

Minister for War in Harold Macmillan's Conservative government, had enjoyed a brief affair with Christine Keeler and had lied about it in a personal statement to Parliament. Profumo's confession, a few months later, blew the lid off a pressure cooker of rumour and allegation hitherto pent-up by draconian English libel law. Many thought the moral fabric of family life was under real threat from this explosion of sexual scandal, and readily identified Stephen Ward as the cause, both factually (he had introduced Profumo to Keeler, and later exposed Profumo's lie to Parliament) and figuratively – he was a successful professional with a promiscuous lifestyle and no belief in God. Punishing him, or at least removing him from the society he had apparently corrupted, offered the possibility of propitiation, even regeneration. In the meantime, casualties of the Profumo affair included the flailing Harold Macmillan, who resigned a few months later, and a failing Tory government, narrowly beaten by Harold Wilson in 1964. Contrary to Lord Hailsham's pompous prediction, a great party *had* been brought down by a confessed liar and a woman of easy virtue.

The choice of Stephen Ward for the role of scapegoat was made by Home Secretary Sir Henry Brooke, who summoned the head of MI5 and the Police Commissioner of Scotland Yard and requested them, in effect, to 'get Ward' – for any offence he could possibly have committed. MI5 baulked when the Home Secretary suggested an Official Secrets Act prosecution – for the very good reason that there was no evidence. The Police Commissioner said there was insufficient evidence for an 'immoral earnings' charge, too, but he volunteered to find some. With unprecedented zeal, the doctor's phones were bugged (with the authorisation of Brooke himself), his home and consulting rooms were put under 24-hour surveillance, and his patients were intercepted by police officers as they left his surgery and asked whether they had witnessed anything improper. Dozens of prostitutes were rounded up and pressured to say bad things about Ward; Keeler herself was interviewed twenty-four times in desperate attempts to implicate him in something felonious.

These efforts produced insufficient evidence of any crime, although the police thought them relevant to some seedy-sounding sexual offences relating to pimping (then called 'poncing') and 'procuring' – abortions, and women for other men. Treasury Counsel (barristers who prosecute for the government) rustled up an indictment, and a rubber-stamp magistrate committed him for trial. It took place over seven days in Court No. 1 at the Old Bailey. Outside, crowds booed and hissed and banged their umbrellas on his car. Inside, the court recoiled as the prosecutor denounced him as a 'thoroughly filthy fellow' and 'an utterly immoral man'. The Lord Chief Justice and two fellow appeal judges arranged that evidence which should have secured his acquittal would be hidden from the jury, and his trial judge misdirected them in a way that led to his conviction on counts of which he was palpably innocent.

Stephen Ward appears now as a British Dreyfus – a reasonable comparison in the sense that both men were innocent victims of public prejudice and politically expedient prosecutions, although at least the Dreyfus affair involved a serious crime that had actually been committed (by someone else), while Ward was charged with crimes for which there was no evidence that he or anyone else had committed. Dreyfus had his champions at the time, like Victor Hugo, who were able to identify the real culprit and secure the victim's release. In Ward's case, there were half a dozen books written at the time and half a dozen which have appeared in the half-century since, and all have condemned the prosecution and the trial. They had been written by journalists – some, outstanding practitioners of that trade, like Ludovic Kennedy and Phillip Knightley, but with limited knowledge of criminal law and procedure. They exposed behaviour that led to a miscarriage of justice, without fully explaining how and why the professional culture at the time allowed the law to produce such a fraudulent result.

The more I studied the case and talked with older barristers and thought back to my own youthful experiences which began at the Old Bailey a few years later, the more it was possible to read between the lines of the journalists' notebooks and court reporters' papers. It struck me that the *Ward* case was an example of what Dr H. V. Evatt, in his analysis of the trial of the Tolpuddle Martyrs, described as 'injustice *within* the law' (*The Tolpuddle Martyrs*, Sydney University Press, 2009 edn). He demonstrated how, at a time of moral or political panic (in that case, at the incipient notion of trade unionism), laws and legal procedures could be manipulated to produce an unjust result notwithstanding a seeming compliance with all forensic formalities.

In Ward's case, the verdict was reached after manipulation – in some respects, disregard – of legal rules in force at the time, and through the legal profession's lack of consciousness then of what fairness in a trial requires. There are quite a few occasions in the following pages where I comment with relief that 'this could not happen now'. Justice in Britain has improved, as a result of the 'Irish miscarriages' (the 'Birmingham Six', the 'Guildford Four' etc.) and the work of Chief Justices like Peter Taylor and Tom Bingham to repair the system that produced them. But trial by jury remains vulnerable, especially at times of moral panic. The importance of quashing the conviction of Stephen Ward is not only to right a historic wrong, but to serve as a warning against unfairly investigating and prosecuting scapegoats in order to expiate scandals which are the responsibility of others who cannot be held to account. Public outrage at the sexual marauding of Jimmy Savile and the tabloid misconduct exposed by Leveson has led to massive police enquiries which are bringing many celebrities, journalists and whistle-blowers into the Old Bailey dock: they *can* be tried fairly, but only if the lessons of Stephen Ward's case have been learnt.

This book began as an idea murmured at the funeral of David Frost, who first appeared on television screens in 1963, that crucible year in which Dr Stephen Ward was tried and convicted. Was it not time, some distinguished mourners wondered, to demand a royal pardon? The discussion was sparked by the presence of Andrew Lloyd Webber, who had become so passionately convinced of Ward's innocence that he had written a musical about him, shortly to be directed by Sir Richard Eyre. Andrew asked my opinion, and I said I would take a look at the case and get back to him. This book is my response.

Geoffrey Robertson QC
Doughty Street Chambers
November 2013

1

HOW TO QUASH AN OLD CONVICTION

Late in the afternoon of Wednesday 31 July 1963, Dr Stephen Ward was convicted at the Old Bailey on two counts alleging that he lived on the earnings of a prostitute, namely those of Christine Keeler (Count 1) and Mandy Rice-Davies (Count 2). He was not in the dock but comatose in hospital. The previous night he had attempted suicide, because (as he said in a note) 'after Marshall's [the judge's] summing-up, I've given up all hope'. He died on Saturday 3 August, without regaining consciousness. Many observers of the proceedings thought the convictions did not reflect the evidence and that the trial was unfair, and this book will show that it breached basic standards of justice, even in 1963 and certainly in 2013.

Unlike most other wrongful convictions, caused by factors like mistaken eyewitnesses, defence incompetence, police malpractice etc., the *Ward* case is so

disturbing because of the role played by the government in initiating it and by the Court of Appeal
(indeed, by the Lord Chief Justice) in hiding from the
Old Bailey jury a crucial fact – that Christine Keeler
was a perjurer – which would have secured Ward's
acquittal, at least on Count 1. These reasons in particular require the verdict, even after half a century, to
be overturned by the Court of Appeal. Not just in the
interest of restoring posthumously Dr Ward's reputation – although there is compelling evidence that he
was innocent of all the offences with which he was
charged – but in the interest of acknowledging how
and why our system of justice buckled under pressure
from politicians and the press and made a scapegoat
of a man who was prosecuted for his promiscuity, and
not for any real criminal offence.

Until 1995, the only means of remedying a wrongful but long past conviction was by way of a royal
pardon, an arcane process which does not overturn
the conviction but formally forgives the crime and
consigns it to legal oblivion.[1] It can still be used for
historic injustices, and was so used in 2006 to pardon
the ghosts of some 300 shell-shocked soldiers executed
during the First World War for crimes of 'cowardice'

---

1   See *R* v. *Foster* [1985] QB 115. 1995 was the year that the
     Criminal Cases Review Commission came into operation.

or 'desertion'. But oblivion is not appropriate for Dr Ward – his unjust conviction deserves not only to be quashed but also to be remembered as a warning to all law enforcers against ever again allowing themselves to be panicked and pressured into giving a citizen an unfair trial.

That the public good would be served by a procedure for examining the correctness of old convictions was accepted by Parliament after a number of miscarriages had done serious damage to the reputation of British justice, particularly jury convictions brought in at a time of public hostility to defendants (the Birmingham Six, the Guildford Four, Judith Ward and others). A Royal Commission, established on the very day in 1991 that the Birmingham Six were released after seventeen years in prison, recommended that there should be a new statutory body, the Criminal Cases Review Commission (CCRC), charged with examining dodgy convictions.[2] It would have special powers to obtain fresh evidence (such as undisclosed prosecution statements or government documents) and to refer a case to the Court of Appeal to reconsider the conviction. This was the means by which Derek Bentley's 'guilty' verdict was quashed, forty-seven

---

2 *Royal Commission on Criminal Justice (Runciman Report)* Cmnd 2263 (1993) pp. 180–87.

years after his execution: Lord Chief Justice Bingham ruled that the conduct of the trial, and the summing-up by Lord Chief Justice Goddard, had been '*such as to deny the appellant a fair trial which is the birth-right of every British citizen*'.[3]

Bentley was a mentally ill young man who had been hanged, despite the jury's recommendation for mercy, for allegedly encouraging his accomplice to shoot a policeman. The quashing of his conviction brought some closure to surviving relatives, but most importantly the Court of Appeal's judgment explained and requited an injustice, perpetrated by a former Chief Justice, which had long disturbed the public conscience. The case of Ruth Ellis (the last woman to be hanged in the UK) was ruled inappropriate for a reference, because there was no dispute that she had killed her perfidious lover,[4] and relatives of Timothy Evans (wrongly convicted in 1950) had their application for a reference turned down because he had already received a royal pardon and the family had been given a six-figure sum in compensation for their grief.[5] In these two cases, clearly there was no

3   *R* v. *Derek William Bentley* [2001] Cr App R 21.
4   *R* v. *Ellis* [2003] EWCA Crim 3556.
5   *Westlake* v. *Criminal Cases Review Commission* [2004] EWHC 2279 (Admin).

further need to right a wrong, and the expense and work involved in a Court of Appeal reference would have little justification. It did, however, in the case of James Hanratty, whose guilt had been disputed ever since his conviction for the 'A6 murder' back in 1961. The CCRC reference forty years later providentially produced DNA evidence to prove his guilt, thus ending a long campaign by journalist Paul Foot, who had written a book arguing for his innocence. The case of Stephen Ward manifestly falls on the Bentley/ Hanratty side of the line: his prosecution has struck all who have investigated it as an appalling misuse of state power, which has never been acknowledged and could, at a future time of moral panic, be repeated.

The CCRC was established by the Criminal Appeal Act of 1995. It is empowered to refer a case to the Court of Appeal if it considers there is a 'real possibility' that the conviction would not, on reconsideration, be upheld.[6] Normally the convictions it refers will already have been dismissed by that court, and of course, back in 1963 Stephen Ward did not and could not appeal – he had taken his own life before the verdict. However, Section 13(2) of the Act permits the commission to make a reference without a previous

---

6   Criminal Appeal Act 1995, Section 13.

appellate judgment if there appear to be 'exceptional circumstances' to justify it. For reasons that will appear, the circumstances of this case could scarcely be more 'exceptional'.

The Court of Appeal must, under guidelines established in Derek Bentley's reference, judge the conduct of the trial and the context of the summing-up according to standards of fairness that apply today, even if they were not recognised at the time of the original trial. However, the statute under which the charges were brought (in Ward's case, Section 30 of the Sexual Offences Act, 1958) must be applied as the law stood in 1963. Under current legal rules and procedures directed to achieving fair trial, there can be no doubt that there is a 'real possibility' – indeed a substantial probability – that the Court of Appeal today would quash this conviction, if the CCRC gives it the opportunity to do so by referring the case.

This book sets out the case for overturning Stephen Ward's conviction, notwithstanding the passage of time. It falls into five parts. The essential background to the trial (Chapter 2) concerns Ward's role in the Profumo affair. The Minister for War had a brief relationship with Christine Keeler at a time when she was living in Ward's flat and was friendly with a Soviet defence attaché, Captain Ivanov. Subsequently, Profumo denied this in a personal statement to Parliament, but was later forced to confess that he had lied and to resign. Harold Macmillan was forced to step down as Prime Minister, and the imbroglio contributed significantly to the Conservatives, who had been in power since 1951, narrowly losing the 1964 election. Ward's role was pivotal: he was living (platonically) with Keeler and introduced her to both Profumo and Ivanov. Later he covered up for the minister, but then told the truth and forced Profumo's resignation.

It is necessary to understand some of this historical background in order to appreciate the forces at work, in Parliament, press and the security services, which came to impinge on the police investigation of Ward and on his trial in July 1963. It is necessary to appreciate that the proceedings began not (as in almost every other criminal case) with a complaint to or action by the police, but with a demand by the Home Secretary, made at a secret meeting with the head of MI5 and the Commissioner of the Metropolitan Police. The police thereafter behaved with extraordinary zeal – never before or since have 140 potential witnesses been interviewed (Keeler twenty-four times) in an effort to drum up evidence against a suspected pimp. Chapter 3 explains how the committal proceedings ensured that some scandalous but inadmissible prosecution evidence was published throughout the world just three weeks before the trial started. I examine the trial itself, with its extraordinary and, as we now know, extraordinarily untruthful evidence, in Chapter 4. It is necessary to analyse the summing-up which drove Ward to suicide, and the machinations of the Court of Appeal which prevented the jury from hearing the truth about Christine Keeler, the prosecution's star witness. In Chapter 5 I set out all the grounds which, separately and together, prove that the trial was unfair – even by the standards of 1963, and certainly by the standards of 2013.

Finally, in Chapter 6, I explain just how appropriate it would be for the CCRC to take up the *Ward* case and to require the Court of Appeal to reconsider it. There are ample grounds which have a 'real possibility' – some of them, a racing certainty – of success. For example:

- It is a rule of our constitution that ministers of the government may not direct the police in operational matters. No minister may tell them who to investigate or who to arrest. Yet, on 27 March 1963, the Home Secretary summoned the head of MI5 and the Commissioner of the Metropolitan Police and asked them whether a criminal prosecution could be brought against Stephen Ward. The head of MI5 replied that there was insufficient evidence for a conviction under the Official Secrets Act. The Commissioner of Police then wondered as to whether he might be charged with living off immoral earnings, and seems to have been directed by the Home Secretary to open an investigation. A few days later, a massive enquiry commenced, under a chief police inspector, involving a round-the-clock watch on Ward's home and consulting room. Patients and friends, numerous prostitutes and former girlfriends were all intrusively interviewed. A prosecution initiated for political purposes by a government minister is an abuse of process.

• Earlier in 1963 Keeler had alleged she had been assaulted by a jilted lover, 'Lucky' Gordon, and she gave evidence to this effect at his trial in order to have him convicted and sentenced to three years' imprisonment. She repeated her lies, under oath, in Ward's trial, which was still going on when Gordon's appeal was heard. The Lord Chief Justice quashed Gordon's conviction, but told Ward's prosecutor and the Old Bailey judge hearing Ward's case that this did not mean that Keeler had lied. The judge told the jury to disregard the overturning of the Gordon conviction. What the Chief Justice did not reveal was that the evidence in the appeal, including

Keeler's tape-recorded confession and the sworn statements of three witnesses, established a compelling case that Keeler had committed perjury – so compelling that she later confessed her guilt and was sentenced to nine months in prison. This evidence on the crucial issue of Keeler's credibility, together with statements on the tape exonerating him from pimping, does not seem to have been disclosed to the Ward defence, and was certainly withheld from the jury which would have been unlikely to convict had they known about it.

• The first, and central, issue for the jury was whether Keeler and Rice-Davies were in fact prostitutes. They denied it, as did Ward. A month before the trial there had been a sensational debate in Parliament, where speakers, beginning with Harold Wilson but continuing from all sides of the House, had labelled them prostitutes, whores and harlots. This characterisation had been widely trumpeted in the press, and large crowds had booed and hissed them outside the court. However, the evidence showed that they fell outside the correct legal definition of prostitute: that of a woman who sold her body 'indiscriminately' or 'arbitrarily' for sex. The judge failed to apply this test, and directed the jury that both Keeler and Rice-Davies could qualify as prostitutes. He failed to warn them against accepting the caricature descriptions bandied about by MPs and the media.

- Ward was charged with living 'in part' on the earnings of prostitutes. The judge gave no direction, as he was required to do, on what this meant, other than telling the jury, wrongly, that it could mean living on merely a fraction of those earnings. The jury might have convicted merely because the women staying at his flat contributed a few pounds to the telephone bill.

- Even if Keeler and Rice-Davies were prostitutes, the evidence established that Ward did not live on their earnings – they lived on his earnings, at a home maintained from his professional practice as an osteopath and his remuneration as an artist.

- A grievous error in the judge's summing-up – the error that appears to have precipitated Ward's suicide – was to tell the jury, twice, that they could infer he was lying under oath because none of his friends – high or low – had come to court to support his defence. In fact, such was the scandal attaching to friendship with Ward in this period that his friends who were asked to testify declined for fear of embarrassment.

- Ward had no previous convictions, and as such was entitled to have the jury directed on his 'good character' – i.e. that this meant he was more likely to be telling the truth and less likely to have committed the offence. Instead, the judge told the jury that he was perplexed and had never been in a situation where a defendant of good character had admitted being of bad character, and indicated that they cancelled each other out. In fact, all that Ward had admitted was a degree of promiscuity: he had enjoyed a number of girl-friends, and several prostitutes, over a three-year period. The judge wrongly thought that these lawful indulgences meant he should be treated as if he was already a convicted criminal.

- The two key witnesses – Keeler and Rice-Davies – had admitted selling their stories for large sums of money. Keeler even admitted adopting, in her evidence, phrases coined for her by a *News of the World* ghost writer, having sold her story for a sum that would now amount to £400,000. In these circumstances it was incumbent on the judge to give a specific warning to the jury against relying on her testimony, unless other evidence convinced them of its truth. He appears to have given no warning at all.

- In any event, as the law then stood, once they had found Keeler and Rice-Davies to be prostitutes the jury could not convict on their evidence unless satisfied that it was 'corroborated', i.e. confirmed, by some untainted independent source. The judge does not appear to have given any direction as to what 'corroboration' meant or any guide as to what evidence could or could not amount to corroboration. This was a requirement of the law in 1963 and failure to give it would require the verdict to be quashed.

- The judge was wrong to proceed with the trial after Ward attempted suicide. The information before the court on the morning after his attempt was that he would not be fit to attend until, at earliest, the following Tuesday, and the judge should in fairness have adjourned the case until then. The danger of sending the jury out that afternoon (by which stage they knew that Ward had made a serious attempt) was that they would interpret this as an admission of guilt, rather than (as was the case) a despairing reaction to an unfair summing-up.

The above grounds of appeal – and there are more – can be advanced by reference to the extensive records of the trial published in books about it in 1963, most notably Ludovic Kennedy's *The Trial of Stephen Ward*. Court No. 1 at the Old Bailey had been packed with journalists and authors taking notes, but its acoustics are poor and their shorthand powers were questionable. The trained official court reporters who sat at a special desk in Court No. 1, a few feet from the judge and the witnesses, heard and took down every word, for transcripts of evidence and summings-up that had always been available for appeal purposes, or for public purchase. Indeed the transcripts of many memorable British trials had been handed over to authors so that their books could be accurate, but Stephen Ward's trial was different. Both Ludovic Kennedy and Wayland Young (Lord Kennet), who were writing books about the trial, applied to purchase the trial transcripts, but their request was referred to the Lord Chief Justice (Lord Parker of Waddington), who refused, without giving reasons.[7] His decision was improper and unprincipled. It was contrary to the 'open justice' rule and gave the impression – correctly, in this case – that the legal system had something to hide. How could it possibly contravene the public interest for an author – or anyone else – to have an accurate copy of directions to the jury, given in public

---

7   See Ludovic Kennedy, 'Letters to Master Thompson', *The Spectator*, 10 January 1964, p. 7.

by a High Court judge? The only reason could be to prevent informed public criticism of that trial judge – an improper reason, given that the whole point of the open justice principle is, as Jeremy Bentham put it, to 'keep the judge, while trying, under trial'.

It is time for the authorities to produce this transcript, copies of which certainly exist, both in the National Archives and among Lord Denning's papers. But go to the National Archives at Kew today, and you will still not be allowed to read the transcript of the evidence or the summing-up, given in public at the Old Bailey, in *R* v. *Ward*. It is the only public trial in British history which is subject to this enforced secrecy, and there can only be one reason, namely to stop researchers from appreciating its unfairness. The reason which is actually given on the file is perverse: it says 'this contains unsubstantiated allegations of prostitution, references to abortions and details of the sexual lives of named individuals'. Quite apart from the fact that all these details were given in open court and reproduced in the press, and quite apart from the fact that these matters are not within any recognised exception for disclosure under the Freedom of Information Act, the allegations of prostitution were certainly not 'unsubstantiated': this was the allegation made in Count 1 and 2 and Ward was convicted of both! Yet as recently as 2011, it was confirmed by some faceless bureaucrat that the official transcript of Britain's most infamous trial would remain inaccessible for eighty-two years – i.e. until 2046. The only exception allows the individuals who actually gave evidence to obtain a copy of the transcript, and Mandy Rice-Davies has taken action under the Freedom of Information Act to obtain her trial testimony. It came with all sorts of threats that she must not disclose it to anyone else, and with all names that she mentioned in open court – Astor, Douglas Fairbanks Jnr and even Christine Keeler – solemnly inked out in heavy black pen by some time- and tax-wasting public servant. Such is the obsession with keeping secret the full truth about the trial of Stephen Ward.

It is time for this absurd secrecy to end, even if the government is determined to keep the Denning file, which also contains the Ward trial transcripts, secret for a century (see Appendix D). The CCRC has special powers to obtain disclosure of documents, and it will have to obtain a copy of the transcript in order to refer the case to the Court of Appeal. That is a further benefit on the road to establishing the truth about the railroading of Stephen Ward.

2

BACKSTORY

Dramatis Personae: Ward, Keeler and Ivanov

Stephen Ward was born in October 1912 (making him fifty at the time of his trial), the second son of a Torquay vicar. After brief studies at the Sorbonne, he spent much of the 1930s at an American university obtaining qualifications as an osteopath. He returned to England on the outbreak of war, when he volunteered for the Royal Army Medical Corps and ended as a commissioned officer in India. Having done the state some service, he took up practice with the Osteopathic Association in London, acquiring his first important and satisfied client, Averell Harriman, the American ambassador. Thereafter came Winston Churchill (with all the status that carried) and others of the Churchill family, Paul Getty, Mahatma Gandhi and various Euroroyals, plus stars like Frank Sinatra, Ava Gardner, Mary Martin and Danny Kaye, and public figures including Sir Malcolm Sargent, Sir Thomas Beecham and Lord Rothermere. He became very friendly with one patient, Lord William 'Bill' Astor, inheritor of Cliveden, the stately home and grounds where his mother, Nancy Astor, had held court between the wars and which had been A. A. Milne's inspiration for Toad Hall in *The Wind in the Willows*. Astor permitted him to occupy, for a peppercorn rent (£1 a year) a cottage on that estate, debouching onto the river. Throughout the 1950s he was a regular guest at Astor soirées at Cliveden, which still attracted a 'Who's Who' of the rich and titled and powerful.

Ward had his consulting rooms at 38 Devonshire Street, near Regent's Park, and a small two-bedroom home (with a garage for his second-hand Jaguar) around the corner at 17 Wimpole Mews. He had married very briefly (it lasted only six weeks) in 1949, and thereafter contented himself with dalliances with young women and what appears to have been an occasional '*nostalgie de la boue*' in the form of sex with streetwalkers. In his spare time he developed a genuine talent for sketching and portraiture: his first exhibition was in July 1960, and he was success-ful enough to obtain a contract from the *Illustrated London News* to draw famous people, and from the *Daily Telegraph* (edited by his friend Sir Colin Coote) to travel to Israel and draw the characters in the Eichmann trial. He became very fashionable – Archbishop Makarios, John Betjeman, Peter Sellers and Sophia Loren all sat for him, and he was invited to Buckingham Palace to sketch Prince Philip and other royals. He socialised with many of his patients and portrait sitters: although often dismissed as a name-dropper, it is clear he had many names to drop. He moved through what counted as high society in London in the 1950s, easing back pain and providing artistic pleasure, often trailing an entourage of attractive young women. There is no evidence that he 'supplied' them to his clients for reward, otherwise it would have been uncovered by police determined to throw the sexual offences book at him in 1963.

Ward stood accused, on Count 1 of his indictment, of living from June 1961 until August 1962 on the immoral earnings of Christine Keeler, 'a common prostitute', at his Wimpole Mews flat. She was, as time would tell, anything but common, despite her humble upbringing in a converted railway carriage near Slough. By age fifteen she was posing for *Titbits*, and had a child the following year (it died a few days after birth) fathered by an American serviceman. She left home and hied up as a dancer at Murray's Cabaret

Club in Soho, posing bare-breasted but (as the law of the time required) motionless. That was where Ward met her, in late 1959, and fell for her in a curious, at least curiously platonic, way. He took her out, drove her home (where her mother encouraged the relationship), took her to Cliveden and commenced what she later described as a 'brother and sister' companionship. From June 1961 to February 1962 she was living with him in Wimpole Mews and spending some weekends with him at Cliveden, where they were often joined by a special friend of Ward's, Captain Ivanov, a Russian spy masquerading as assistant naval attaché at the Soviet embassy.[8]

Yevgeny (Eugene) Ivanov had been introduced to Ward by the editor of the *Daily Telegraph* at a luncheon at the Garrick Club in January 1961, and the two became good friends. Ward's politics were egalitarian and vaguely left-wing (in a 'champagne socialist' way) and his dazzling array of patients and portrait sitters made him a perfect contact for the sociable spy. When MI5 began to tail Ivanov (as the latter expected they would), they discovered his trail often led to

---

8   Phillip Knightley and Caroline Kennedy, *An Affair of State: The Profumo Case and the Framing of Stephen Ward* (Jonathan Cape, 1987), p. 74. Ivanov's espionage role was unmasked to MI6 by Oleg Penkovsky, a fellow GRU officer who was executed for spying for the British.

Ward's door at Wimpole Mews. Ivanov was significant, because his wife's father was President of the Soviet Supreme Court and his conviviality and familiarity with the English language would make him a useful double-agent, or possibly even a defector. There is evidence that the reason MI5 recruited Ward was to help 'turn' him. A high-level decision was taken by its officials in early June 1961 to ask Ward's help, at least to keep an eye on Ivanov and, if the occasion arose, to participate in an operation to get Ivanov to defect. At MI5's initiative, a luncheon was arranged between 'Mr Woods of room 393 of the War Office' (in fact, MI5 officer Keith Wagstaffe) and Ward. It took place on 8 June 1961. Afterwards, Ward invited 'Woods' back to Wimpole Mews for tea, which was served, so he reported, by 'the most beautiful woman I have ever clapped eyes on' – Christine Keeler.

The jury at Ward's trial would have been fascinated to learn that MI5 was in touch with Ward at the very time and place where he was alleged to be living off this tea lady's earnings, and how he later reported to them some details of the relationships between Profumo and Keeler and Ivanov and Keeler. But by the time of his trial in 1963, when his solicitor was desperately looking for witnesses, 'Mr Woods from the War Office' was not returning calls.

The Cliveden Weekend

The pieces were now in place for an iconic moment in British political and sexual history – the Cliveden weekend of 8–9 July 1961. Nancy Astor's 'Cliveden Set' in the 1930s had been a fabled crucible of upper-class influence, and her son affected to maintain the tradition. His guest of honour was Field Marshal Ayub Khan, President of Pakistan, en route to Washington for a meeting with President Kennedy. Invited to surround him were John Profumo, Minister of State for War with his celebrated actress wife Valerie Hobson (*Kind Hearts and Coronets*), together with Lord Mountbatten, Sir Robert Lancaster and the government's economic adviser Sir Roy Harrod, plus a few socialite aristocrats, a Polish countess and a fashionable interior designer. While they feasted in 'The Big House', down by the riverbank cottage lay Stephen Ward and his new flame Sally Norie, with Christine Keeler and another attractive woman they had picked up at a bus stop on the way down. It was a hot summer night, and the river-bankers made their way up to the swimming pool, which Ward had a standing invitation to use, and began disporting themselves late into the evening.

After supper, the dinner-jacketed guests took a post-prandial stroll: Profumo and Astor were the first to clap eyes on Christine, naked but for a hand towel. The scene has been replayed so often, and with so many embellishments, that it is difficult to tell what really happened next, other than that she was introduced, with some embarrassment, to the President of Pakistan and (with more) to Mrs Profumo. The Ward entourage was invited back the next day, when they brought Captain Ivanov, who had joined them that morning. They had swimming races in the pool (Profumo won, by cheating) and a good time was had by all except the President of Pakistan, who had to leave for Washington. Profumo was later to tell Lord Denning that 'all the girls were very young, and very pretty and very common',[9] presumably in ascending order of attraction, because he took Christine Keeler aside to give her a personal tour of the mansion, and then asked Ward for her phone number (which, of course, was Ward's as well).

Ward stayed at the cottage that evening while Keeler and Ivanov motored back to Wimpole Mews, where they polished off a bottle of vodka and may or may not have had sex. That they did depends on the word of Christine Keeler, written for her by a *News of the World* journalist and published shortly before

---

9   Richard Davenport-Hines, *An English Affair: Sex, Class, and Power in the Age of Profumo* (Collins, 2013), p. 250.

Ward's trial, for a massive inducement of £23,000, which would amount today to £400,000:

> He was like a God ... clumsy perhaps but only because he wanted me ... what had happened between us was something as old as time ... I could sense his sadness, the deep, black gloom that I am told all Russians feel ... I never dreamed I might be the girl who rocked the government ... I know nothing of high affairs, all I know is that when I allowed Eugene to love me I was young and free.

If inebriated intercourse did follow, there was no suggestion that Ivanov paid her for it, so the encounter was not discussed at Ward's trial, although Keeler's story gave rise to endless sensationalism in the press and Parliament, and to the bogus claim that national security was at stake because a government minister was sharing a woman's bed with a Russian spy. This claim – the mainspring of the Profumo affair – would not emerge for eighteen months, embellished with elements of classic farce (the ministerial car draws up at the front door as the Russian spy leaves by the back) masquerading as a matter of national security. What is interesting, in terms of whether Ward was living off Keeler's immoral earnings in this 'Count 1' period, is that on the following Monday he called 'Woods', his MI5 case officer, and met him on the Wednesday, to report that Ivanov had met Profumo, that he had been binge-drinking (not lovemaking) with Keeler, and had asked Ward to find out when the US was going to supply West Germany with nuclear weapons.[10] Ward was being useful to the security services, which were seriously considering a 'defection' operation (although not, as some journalists have suggested, a 'honey trap' with Keeler as its bait), and MI5 has now admitted, in its 'authorised' history published in 2009, that Ward was being used by the Foreign Office as a back channel to pass information through Ivanov to the Soviets. This would have been useful information for a jury in judging the patriotic character of a defendant whom Harold Wilson had smeared as a 'Soviet intermediary' and whom the prosecution said was running Keeler at this time as a prostitute. She was, in fact, soon running herself quite proficiently as the girlfriend of a government minister.

She had fallen in love with a law student friend of Ward's, Noel Howard-Jones, who had bedded her a few times and then cooled because she had no big talk and he found her 'dull in bed'. So she had no romantic relationship on the go in the summer of 1961 which would deter her dalliance with the War Minister. Profumo had sex with her, during Ward's absence,

---

10   Knightley and Kennedy, *An Affair of State*, p. 87.

in his Wimpole Mews flat and on one occasion, when
his wife was absent, at his Regent's Park home. Their
liaison lasted for a few months, during a period when
the Crown at Ward's trial would allege she was a
prostitute. But there was never any deal between her
and Profumo that he would pay for his pleasure – on
one occasion he gave her, post-coitally, a cigarette
lighter, and on another, £20 – 'a little something for
your mother'. She did not hand this money to Ward.
She was occupying a bedroom in his house without
paying rent. Yet this £20 became part of the Crown's
evidence that he was 'living in part on her earnings as
a prostitute'. There would be payments by only two
other lovers before she moved out in February 1962,
an old friend called Mr Eynan, to whom she had not
been introduced by Ward, and on one occasion by a
man called 'Charles' whom we now know to have
been the property developer Charles Clore. She took
with her one fateful memento of her 'high affair' – a
letter on War Office notepaper postponing a tryst,
addressed to her as 'Darling' and signed 'J'.

Ward, throughout this Count 1 period, maintained
his workaday practice as an osteopath, and his quite
lucrative hobby as a portrait painter and illustrator.
Weekends were spent at the Cliveden cottage, where
he cultivated the garden (his pride and joy) as well as

relationships with attractive (and always consenting and unmarried) young women. Back in London there were fleeting resorts to prostitutes, and occasional attendances at dinner parties which may have featured a masked 'slave' or group sex as an hors d'oeuvre. But his most common social activity was bridge – he often had 'foursomes' (always men) to play into the early hours of the morning, with Christine (and subsequently Mandy) to make coffee. This aspect of his domestic routine went unmentioned by the prosecution at his trial.

In one respect, the louche curiosity of a man commonly described, in the argot of the time, as a 'gay bachelor', was to have disastrous consequences for both him and Keeler. He had taken to dropping in to Notting Hill jazz cafes, the haunt of West Indian musicians and cannabis smokers, in order to sketch their black bohemian faces. Christine came along, or may have taken him there, and was soon buying marijuana from a singer, Aloysius 'Lucky' Gordon, and later having sex with him, and then with his rival Johnny Edgecombe, with whom she lived for a while after leaving the mews. Ward was strongly opposed to her regular smoking of cannabis, so much so that when he caught her doing it at Wimpole Mews he marched her down to Scotland Yard for a lecture from a drugs squad officer (which would have been unusual behaviour for a man accused of being her pimp). It was one of the disputes that led to her departure from the mews and to her difficult and dangerous life in the following years, sandwiched between two aggressive and possessive black lovers. Edgecombe at one point (October 1962) knifed Gordon in a fight over her, and when Keeler left him and briefly returned to stay at Wimpole Mews in December, he turned up outside with a loaded gun and pumped bullets into the door. By that time Mandy Rice-Davies was in residence, on whose earnings as a prostitute Ward was now alleged to be living.

Mandy Rice-Davies – The Count 2 Period

Mandy Rice-Davies had indeed come to live with Stephen Ward, in this 'Count 2' period between September and December 1962. She was the daughter of a Birmingham policeman and had left home at sixteen to join the showgirls at Murray's Cabaret Club, where she became friendly with the older (by two years) Christine Keeler. The two frequently shared lodgings, and it was not long before Mandy was part of the Ward entourage, pictured with him at Cliveden in June 1961. She had sex (but only once) with Ward at the cottage and maintained a friendship until falling out in early 1963. From mid-1961 to November 1962 she was the reasonably faithful mistress of Peter Rachman, the 'slum landlord' of Notting Hill, who set her up with an income of £80 per week and a flat which had a broken two-way mirror that came to feature often in Ward's trial for no better reason than that he had once made a joke about it. She had hoped to marry Rachman, who had made unfulfilled promises to divorce his wife, and she asked to stay with Ward in October 1962 after a quarrel over Rachman's breach of promise. She still loved him, however, and fainted when Ward broke the news to her a few weeks later that he had suddenly died from a heart attack. (Maliciously, Ward could not resist telling people that she came round long enough to ask 'did he leave a will?') Nonetheless, in grief – whether at his death, or her lack of a legacy, or both – she took an overdose of sleeping pills and was rushed to hospital. Ward invited her parents to stay with him at Wimpole Mews to nurse her when she was discharged.

It was Ward's introduction of Mandy to a man whose name was suppressed at the trial (he was called 'the Indian doctor') which was to feature as the prosecutor's main (indeed only) evidence on Count 2. He was, in fact, the Ceylonese conman Emil Savundra. A few years later, Savundra achieved brief notoriety as David Frost's victim of what the Court of Appeal called 'trial by television' and received a prison sentence after trial by jury, for an insurance swindle. In October 1962 he fell for Mandy, shortly after she moved to the mews to assert her independence from Rachman. Savundra sent her forests of flowers and arranged to meet her twice a week at the mews, paying £25 (the cost of her weekly drama lessons) and similar sums for enjoying her favours at lunchtimes, while Ward was at his surgery. She indulged him enjoyably on half a dozen occasions, and he left her money whether they had sex or not. But she tired of him after a fortnight and the relationship ended.

In mid-December, with Mandy just recovered from the suicide bid after nursing from her parents, Christine came back to the mews house for refuge and Johnny Edgecombe came to find her – with a loaded gun. He shot five bullets into the door when Mandy refused him admittance. It was lunchtime; Ward was at his surgery, but called the police when the neighbours rang with the news. Edgecombe was soon caught and charged – not only with possession of an unlicensed firearm, but with shooting with intent to cause grievous bodily harm to Keeler. The press coyly reported that 'Miss Keeler, 20, a freelance model, was visiting Miss Marilyn Davies, an actress, at Dr Ward's home.'

1962 came and went, its heaviest shadow being the Cuban missile crisis in October. Ward, at Ivanov's request, passed on to his Foreign Office friends the suggestion that Britain should act as an honest broker and resolve the crisis by hosting a meeting between Khrushchev and Kennedy. It was not a bad idea, canvassed by others at the time, but Ward's special contribution was to pass on Ivanov's guarantee that Khrushchev would attend. He was, for this effort, condemned by press and politicians just before his trial as a 'Soviet intermediary', which was hardly fair. The idea would have undercut Kennedy's posture of intransigence, which the Foreign Minister (Lord Home) insisted on supporting, but Ward obviously believed he was making a 'peace initiative' and it is wrong to describe him (as MPs did in debates before his trial) as a 'Communist sympathiser' or 'Soviet agent'. Ward was always happy to serve the ruling class, so long as their laissez-faire attitudes permitted the libertarianism in his private life. He thought himself patriotic in helping MI5 and in making well-intentioned peace initiatives which would boost Britain's role in the world. The *noblesse oblige* class with whom he mingled gave him every reason to believe he was valued, but he did not mix with the class that ruled the law – judges and prosecutors who practised what they preached, namely a low-church moral puritanism which believed promiscuity should be punished in life as well as after death. This was the caste that ruled the courts in 1963, and was soon to get its hands on Stephen Ward. He was described by his prosecutor, with lofty moral disdain, as 'a thoroughly filthy fellow' and with venom by Lord Denning (who had in his time sentenced murderers and poisoners) as 'the most evil man I have ever met'.

Rumour-mongering

That meeting was yet to come. Christine Keeler, at loose in a world of drugs and petty crime and popular newspapers, was talking and telling her story at Christmas parties and soon found an agent who began to peddle it, for money, around Fleet Street tabloids. In January 1963 it reached the ears of George Wigg MP, Harold Wilson's security adviser and shadow Army Minister, who had political scores to settle with Profumo. Keeler offered the 'Darling' letter to the *Sunday Pictorial*, which paid her £200 on the spot. (All sums of money in this period must be multiplied many times to find a modern equivalent: £1 in 1963 equalled £17.75 in 2013.) It was the beginning of a lucrative trade which ended with the £23,000 (i.e. £400,000) deal with the *News of the World,* in which the sensation of receiving that amount of money would have to match the sensations in the story. In her tabloid tale, Ivanov became her lover and had asked her to find out from her other lover, Jack Profumo, exactly when the US was going to supply nuclear weapons to West Germany. The question was otiose (US nuclear weapons were already in West Germany) and the notion that this question could ever pass as pillow talk was ridiculous. But in London's small media-political world, this was a pressure cooker of scandal, waiting, from January of 1963, to explode.

British libel law was, at this time, draconian. The UK did not have free speech, it had expensive speech. A recent case, in which the thuggish Labour MP John Lewis had been awarded £100,000 for a true report in the *Daily Telegraph* that Scotland Yard's fraud squad had commenced an inquiry into his company, had sent a chill down editorial spines. There was no public interest defence for imputations that lowered a chap in the estimation of right-minded gentle-men, and the only way of getting out to the public a story of public importance that powerful forces wanted to stop was to have it spoken by an MP under parliamentary privilege – the device that had been used to expose Kim Philby as a Soviet spy. The government admitted the truth of this allegation on 1 July, adding to the general climate of hysteria surrounding Ward's trial which opened three weeks later.

The press had particular problems with the government at this time: in February, two reporters were jailed for refusing to disclose their sources to the Vassall Inquiry into another spy scandal, and the anger on Fleet Street was intense. All newspapers knew, by the end of January, about Profumo's affair and the Ivanov triangle, but were afraid to publish. Christine even told her story to Detective Sergeant Burrows on 26 January, when he made a courtesy call at the mews to remind her to attend court as a witness in the forthcoming trial of Johnny Edgecombe (the man who had shot at the Wimpole Mews door and was now charged with attempting to kill her). For a reason that subsequently Lord Denning (who reported on the security aspects of the Profumo affair) was unable to fathom, but was probably incompetence, the fact that Christine had told the police about her affair with Profumo was not passed on to MI5 or the Attorney-General. Throughout February, lawyers for both Profumo and Ward were engaged, successfully, with keeping the story out of various newspapers by threatening action for libel and by attempting to buy off Keeler and her lawyer. Profumo asked MI5 to issue a 'D' notice on her story (sensibly they declined) and then asked the DPP to prosecute Keeler for blackmail when her lawyer asked £5,000 for withdrawing her memoir (sensibly, he declined). With much less sense, the law officers, Attorney-General Sir John Hobson and Sir Peter Rawlinson, the Solicitor General, took Profumo's word that he had not been interested in sex with Christine – without asking him what *had* so interested him that they dated over several months. Ivanov, meanwhile, had the good sense to leave Britain in a hurry at the end of January – the KGB, but not the Macmillan government, could predict what was to come.

On 14 March, the opening day of Edgecombe's trial for attempting to kill Keeler, the would-be murder victim failed to attend court. It was packed with journalists hoping for some mention of her affair with Profumo. Instead of adjourning or issuing a warrant for her arrest, the judge allowed the prosecution to drop this serious charge and proceed only on a count of possessing an unlicensed firearm, on which Edgecombe was convicted and sentenced to an extraordinarily severe seven-year imprisonment. So 'where was Christine?' the tabloids asked on their front pages, adorned with photographs of 'the missing witness' in her bikini. She had, on her own initiative, taken a holiday in Spain, but the Westminster rumour mill whispered that Profumo must have had something to do with her 'disappearance'. On 21 March, *Private Eye*'s political correspondent 'Lunchtime O'Booze' had a historic scoop:

IDLE TALK

Mr Silas Jones, a West Indian immigrant of no fixed abode, was today sentenced at the Old Bailey to twenty-four years' Preventative Detention for being in possession of an offensive water pistol.

The chief 'witness' in the case, gay, fun-loving Miss Gaye Funloving, a 21-year-old 'model', was not actually present in Court. She has, in fact, disappeared. It is believed that normally, in cases of this type, a Warrant is issued for the arrest of the missing witness.

'PARTIES'

One of Miss Funloving's close 'friends', Dr Spook of Harley Street, revealed last night he could add nothing to what had already been insinuated.

Dr Spook is believed to have 'more than half the Cabinet on his list of patients'. He also has a 'weekend' cottage on the Berkshire estate of Lord —, and is believed to have attended many 'parties' in the neighbourhood.

Among those it is believed have also attended 'parties' of this type is Mr Vladimir Bolokhov, the well-known Soviet spy attached to the Russian embassy, and a well-known Cabinet minister.

RESIGNATION?

Mr James Montesi, a well-known Cabinet minister, was last night reported to have proffered his 'resignation' to the Prime Minister, on 'personal grounds'.

It is alleged that the Prime Minister refused to accept his alleged 'resignation'. Mr Montesi today denied the allegations that he had ever allegedly offered his alleged 'resignation' to the alleged 'Prime Minister'.

Profumo's Parliamentary Denial

The chill created by the libel laws could only be side-stepped by using parliamentary privilege. At 11 p.m. on the day of the *Private Eye* report, Colonel Wigg rose from the Labour benches in the House of Commons to 'rightly use the privilege of the House – that is what it is given to me for' to ask the Home Secretary to deny rumours heard and now read by every MP and Press Gallery journalist 'relating to Miss Christine Keeler and Miss Davies and a shooting by a West Indian'. Richard Crossman and Barbara Castle (who described Keeler as 'a call girl') followed, and this sanctimonious Labour onslaught was broken only by Mr Reginald Paget: 'These rumours amount to the fact that a minister is said to be acquainted with an extremely pretty girl ... I should have thought that was a matter for congratulation rather than enquiry.' Nobody else thought like that, and the government whips realised that it was time to bite the bullet.

After the debate – at two in the morning – the party whip summoned Profumo from his bed to attend the House, with his solicitor, and to sign off on a 'personal statement' which he would have to make to Parliament the next morning. Five ministers surrounded the wretched man as he passionately maintained that his relationship with Keeler had never involved sex, although any streetwise person would realise it involved little else. The credulous Tory colleagues overlooked the 'Darling' letter, which he explained on the basis that through his wife he mixed with theatre people, who all called each other 'darling'. The two law officers, Hobson and Rawlinson, retired with Profumo's personal solicitor to draft his 'personal statement' – a serious mistake on their part, because they were undermining the constitutional independence of their office in order to help a personal friend and, of course, to stop their own party being mired in scandal. They actually drafted his 'personal statement', as if they were barristers retained to act for him, at a two-hour session with his solicitor from which Profumo and the other ministers were excluded.

Although Profumo agreed with it, the statement was written by and for the government and was calculated to give impressions that were misleading: 'My wife and I had a standing invitation to visit Dr Ward. Between July and December 1962 I met Miss Keeler on about half a dozen occasions at Dr Ward's flat, when I called to see him and his friends. Miss Keeler and I were on friendly terms.' The veiled suggestion that Mrs Profumo was with him on these occasional visits, where Christine just happened to be present among Ward's other friends, was a misleading spin-doctoring of Profumo's admission that he had visited the mews to see her. There was no mention of the 'Darling' letter, which both law officers had been told about. Denning later claimed that it was a 'well-accepted convention' that a minister of the Crown was entitled to consult the law officers over whether he should bring an action, but it is neither 'well accepted' nor a 'convention' that they should act as his private lawyers and draft a misleading personal statement for him. Their behaviour helped to identify the government with the lies and half-truths it contained. These were the circumstances in which the government's anger was to turn, not so much against the political opportunism of Wigg and Wilson, but against the man who would soon blow the whistle on a carefully constructed cover-up.

That man was Stephen Ward. In Profumo's personal statement, which he read to a packed and hushed House a few hours later, with his wife in the gallery and Prime Minister Macmillan loyally by his side, he declared:

> There was no impropriety whatsoever in my acquaintanceship with Miss Keeler. I shall not hesitate to issue writs for libel and slander if scandalous allegations are made or repeated outside the House.

After these fighting words, Profumo and his wife went to Sandown races and were photographed with the Queen Mother, the ultimate symbol of respectability. Keeler, discovered in Spain, was paid to give Profumo's personal statement an equivocal endorsement. ('Ours was a friendship no one could criticise.') Ward popped up on television to lend it some credibility.

('I was there. Nothing of a sinister nature happened.') Profumo then made good his threat and actually sued an Italian magazine which suggested the contrary: cowed by English libel law, it made a payment into court which he publicly donated to an army charity. For the next two months, to the fury of editors and journalists, he had to be portrayed to the public as a man of unblemished repute – any statement of the obvious would incur heavy damages. Perhaps he would have got away with it, had the grandees in his party not decided to punish, or at least to silence, Stephen Ward, perceived as the cause of all his – and their – problems. On 26 March, Ward was observed in a lengthy meeting with George Wigg in a tearoom in the House of Commons. He talked about his MI5 connections, and said he had notified them, the week after Cliveden, of Profumo's interest in Keeler.

The Home Secretary Calls the Police

The very next day, Home Secretary Henry Brooke and his permanent undersecretary (Sir Charles Cunningham) summoned the head of MI5 (Roger Hollis) and the Commissioner of the Metropolitan Police (Sir Joseph Simpson) to a curious, and constitutionally improper, meeting. The full transcript has never been released, but the Denning Report confirms that the meeting took place. Denning says it was prompted by rumours that MI5 had been sending anonymous letters to Mrs Profumo – a ridiculous idea, and in any case a matter which hardly needed a meeting with the Home Secretary and the Metropolitan Police Commissioner. What the Home Secretary did ask Hollis – obviously the real reason for the meeting – was whether Ward could be prosecuted under the Official Secrets Act. Hollis replied that the witnesses were unreliable and there would be little chance of conviction. The Home Secretary then turned to Simpson and 'asked whether there was a police interest' in Ward – i.e. whether they could prosecute him. According to Denning, Simpson replied that there might be 'if the police were able to get the full story' but he doubted whether they would succeed. It might, so he said in other accounts, be possible to get him for 'immoral earnings'.

It would seem that the Home Secretary, described later by Hollis as 'excitable' at this meeting, was conveying the message that he wanted a law enforcement agency to investigate and prosecute Stephen Ward. Hollis went away to consider further whether there were any Official Secrets Act possibilities: he took legal advice, which confirmed his negative view. Simpson went away to order a police investigation under Chief Inspector Samuel Herbert, which began by interviewing Christine Keeler on 4 April. 'Get Ward' was the message the Home Secretary must have conveyed to the Police Commissioner on 27 March, and it was now being acted upon only because the Home Secretary had sent it. It is not known what instructions the Commissioner gave to Mr Herbert to put Ward in the frame, although officers in the team said much later that they were told that if the operation was successful they would receive promotions, 'but not immediately because it would not look good'.[11]

Although final judgment on the 27 May meeting must await release of the official minutes, it does raise a serious constitutional issue relating to the power of ministers to give operational directions to the police. Authors who have investigated Henry Brooke's conduct suggest that he acted because Ward was seen blabbing to Wigg in the tearoom the day before, and in the belief that the Profumo affair would only end once Ward was forced to shut up. The threat of criminal prosecution would cower him, and if a prosecution did go ahead successfully it would serve to discredit whatever he had to say about Profumo. Others regard it as more probable that Brooke, a fervent Christian but poor tactician, acted out of

11   Quoted by Knightley and Kennedy, *An Act of State*, p. 254. The two senior police officers were in fact promoted.

moral disgust – he wanted Ward put away because he set a rotten example for youth, making young women available to tempt old Tories. Whatever the reason for his action, Brooke abused his powers if he directed the police to 'get Ward' – and his behaviour at the meeting undoubtedly led to Ward's investigation and subsequent prosecution. If his motive was to protect the government from Ward's loose tongue, it was not only an unconstitutional act, but one of monumental political stupidity, because a show trial of Ward would inevitably show that Profumo had lied to Parliament.

Profumo Confesses

In the end, and ironically, it was Ward's struggle against an oppressive police investigation that tightened the screws on Profumo until he confessed. In order to find something to pin on Ward, they had by early May set up a 24-hour watch on his home and office, and his telephone had been tapped, necessarily with the Home Secretary's approval. (That approval should not have been given for an investigation of a minor crime, but Brooke did not believe Ward to be a minor criminal.) The police team interrogated 140 potential witnesses, and Inspector Herbert threatened prostitute Ronna Ricardo that her child would be taken into care and her sister arrested if she did not make a statement against

Ward. When Mandy Rice-Davies refused to cooperate, Herbert had her arrested for carrying a false driving licence. She was denied bail and held in Holloway for nine days – until she was ready to talk. The police went further and interviewed Ward's friends (Astor found this a deeply embarrassing experience) and stood ostentatiously outside his professional rooms in Devonshire Street, asking patients as they left whether the osteopath had made any improper suggestions. This quickly destroyed his practice, and Ward determined to fight back. He told friends, who advised him to keep quiet, that he had once been badly beaten by teachers at his private school after covering up for the real culprit: he was not going to take the blame again.

At first – and it is a measure of the naivety of the man – Ward thought he could call in a government favour, because he had until now covered up for Profumo. On 7 May he regaled the Prime Minister's private secretary with 'explosive material' – his knowledge of the liaison – which he threatened to make public if the police bloodhounds were not called off. Quite rightly, he was shown the door. On 19 May, he wrote to the Home Secretary complaining that the police questioning of his patients was damaging him professionally and that malicious complaints were being made 'because I have done what I could do to shield Mr Profumo from his indiscretion'.

The reply came the next day: 'The Home Secretary has asked me to explain that the police, in making whatever inquiries they think proper, do not act under his direction.'

This was a 'very proper' response said Denning later (his report was not published until September). It was also a pretty rich one, since the police action against Ward had only begun at the Home Secretary's exhortation, at his meeting with the Commissioner on 27 March.

But Ward was not going quietly – he was going to take Profumo with him. He copied his letter to the Home Secretary to all newspaper editors. But still terrified by Profumo's libel threat, they refused to publish. Then he wrote to Harold Wilson asserting that Profumo had not told the truth and he no longer wished to cover up for him. Macmillan, hounded by Wilson and Wigg for having a Minister of War who was a security risk (they believed the rumour that Ivanov was having sex with Keeler at the same time as she was going to bed with Profumo), then asked the Lord Chancellor, Viscount Dilhorne, to begin an inquiry. Profumo flew to Venice for a short holiday with his wife before facing cross-examination by Dilhorne (formerly Reginald Manningham-Buller QC, known unaffectionately at the Bar as Reginald

Bullying-Manner). After dinner on their first night at the Cipriani, Profumo confessed. As Denning tells it, 'Mrs Profumo said, "Oh darling. We must go home now as soon as we can and face up to it."' This is probably an over-romantic version of Profumo's volte-face – the net had closed, and a jostling crowd of reporters and photographers at London airport as he left told him his time was up. He could face down the cash-induced Keeler stories, but not the solemn statements of a well-connected doctor. Stephen Ward's letters to the press forced Profumo's resignation and certainly forced him to tell his wife. His resignation letter was delivered to the Prime Minister on 4 June 1963.

3

HUNTING UP EVIDENCE

'Lucky' Gordon: Keeler Commits Perjury

The initially unheard overture to Stephen Ward's trial was played as early as 17 April 1963, when Keeler was living with a friend, Paula Hamilton-Marshall. She had a furious row with Paula's brother, John: he reacted by hitting her hard, leaving a black eye and facial bruises. Some hours later, her rejected ex-lover 'Lucky' Gordon came banging on her door, but was stopped by two other West Indians, named Fenton and Comacchio, who refused him entry. Keeler called the police, but falsely told them she had been assaulted by Gordon, who was soon arrested and charged with causing her grievous bodily harm. It was, it turned out, a false allegation.[12]

---

12 Knightley and Kennedy suggest she was put up to it by Herbert, who wanted to trap Gordon into making a statement against Ward by offering to drop the bogus charge of assaulting Keeler. See *An Affair of State*, pp. 170–71.

Gordon was brought to trial at the Old Bailey on 5 June – the day after Profumo's resignation. Keeler, now the focus of world as well as *News of the World* attention, turned up dressed in fashionable mauve, and stepped from a Rolls Royce to give perjured evidence that would secure Gordon a three-year prison sentence. Gordon had defended himself, accusing Keeler of infecting him with venereal disease – at which she screamed abuse and had to be removed from court. Gordon asked that the men who restrained him from beating her up at the very time he was charged with beating her up – Fenton and Comacchio – should be called as eyewitnesses to his innocence, but the police told the court that they could not be traced. (This was curious, at least in relation to Comacchio, who had been remanded on bail to a fixed address.) In their absence, and perhaps because a person who defends himself sometimes does have a fool for a client, Gordon was convicted of assaulting Keeler and sentenced to three years in prison. He would soon have powerful grounds of appeal: Fenton and Comacchio came forward to make witness statements, and so did John Hamilton-Marshall who actually confessed to committing the crime.

Gordon's grounds for appeal became even more

compelling with the emergence of a lengthy tape recording made by Keeler with her former 'manager', a Mr Robin Durie. It lasted ten hours, and included admissions that Gordon had not assaulted her and had been 'set up' to take the blame. It also contained comments helpful to Ward – that the investigation was attempting to frame him, that the police were 'trying to persuade me to say something against Stephen' and so on. Durie refused to disclose it to anyone, but a journalist who had access to it sent a transcript of some sections to George Wigg MP, who passed this on to the Attorney-General, John Hobson QC. It was the latter's duty to disclose this to Ward's prosecutors, the Treasury Counsel at the Old Bailey, who should in turn have disclosed it to the defence, but this did not happen. Hobson sent the extracts to the DPP, Sir Theo Mathew, who realised that the tape would assist Gordon's appeal and asked the Court of Criminal Appeal to use its powers to order Durie to produce it. On 15 July, just a week before the beginning of Ward's trial, that is precisely what the court did. But it was a curious hearing. The *Criminal Law Review* commented on 'an air of discreet allusiveness' in the court presided over by the Chief Justice. Names were not mentioned, and 'the impression of secretiveness which was created was not obviously appropriate to a hearing in open court.'[13] The order was that the DPP should transcribe the tape and send this transcription to the court, which would view and edit it so that only *the part of the tape that the judges thought relevant* would be provided to Gordon's defenders. The judges – Lord Chief Justice Parker, Justice Widgery (a future Chief Justice) and Justice Sachs seemed to be taking extreme steps to ensure that only extracts relevant to Gordon's case – and not further extracts that might be relevant to Ward's case – would see the light of day. The tape was retrieved from a bank vault and taken by Sergeant Burrows to Scotland Yard for transcription.[14]

Ward is Arrested

Ward was arrested on Saturday 8 June, the day after unlucky Gordon was sentenced to prison. The next day, Sunday, was the first time the *News of the World* was free to publish the Keeler confessions: Profumo had admitted his 'guilt', so was no longer a libel risk. The confessions, for which it had paid a fortune, were massively prejudicial to Ward, depicting him as a lecher

---

13   'The Appeal of Aloysius Lincoln Gordon', *Criminal Law Review*, September 1963, p. 600.

14   Iain Crawford, *The Profumo Affair* (White Lodge, 1963), pp. 128–9.

and a crypto-Soviet agent. He was refused bail, and was kept in prison for almost a month – a development both cruel and sinister. The man had a successful professional life, with no previous convictions, and the charges were not of violent crime. He was entitled to bail, but the feeling against him, even in the lowly magistrates' court, was so intense that he could not receive the most basic right of a person presumed to be innocent.

That right was further jeopardised in the great debate in Parliament on 17 June over the Profumo affair. It was a landmark moment in British political history, a 'debate without precedent in the annals of this House', as Labour's new leader Harold Wilson said in opening it. He eviscerated the mournful Macmillan, whose failing government had closed ranks to protect a man who had committed the ultimate political sin – lying, in a personal statement to Parliament. During the debate, time and again, it was asserted as a fact that Keeler was a prostitute – she was described as such, and as a 'harlot' and a 'tart' and a 'whore'. The very first question for Ward's jury to decide, in a few weeks' time, would be whether Christine Keeler was any of those words, because if she wasn't, Ward could not be convicted of living on her earnings. His jury were having their minds made up beforehand, by MPs whose characterisation of her was echoed in every newspaper and on every television news programme.

What was worse was the constant vilification of a man whom all MPs knew was about to stand trial. Harold Wilson constantly referred to him as a 'Soviet intermediary', and a representative of 'a diseased existence, a corrupted and poisoned appendix of a small section of society'. Noting a news story that Christine Keeler ('or should I refer to her as 'Miss Christine Keeler Ltd') had just incorporated herself for tax reasons and been offered £5,000 a week to appear at a nightclub, he went on: 'I say to the Prime Minister that there is something utterly nauseating about a system of society which pays a harlot twenty-five times as much as it pays its Prime Minister, 250 times as much as it pays its MPs and 500 times as much as it pays its ministers of religion.' Tories were no less indignant – Viscount Lambton actually spoke of 'The treason of Dr Ward', who was 'in close touch with the highest of Soviet circles'. He lamented the fact that 'the Minister for War had been in close touch with a spy, with a semi-Soviet agent and with a girl in the prostitution racket'. (It is difficult to resist reference to the irony that Lord Lambton, when himself a defence minister a few years later, was caught in bed with *two* 'girls in the prostitution racket' and a large reefer, the latter (according to the Diplock Report) rendering him likely to talk unguardedly to Soviet agents.) George Wigg, who also spoke demeaningly of Ward in the debate, was arrested years later for kerb-crawling in Oxford Street (he said he was looking for a newspaper, and was acquitted).

The Committal Hearing

On 28 June the 'preliminary hearing' began at Marylebone Magistrates' Court, to determine whether there was sufficient evidence to commit Ward for trial. This was an arcane and unfair procedure, now abolished, which allowed all the Crown's prejudicial evidence, whether admissible at the trial or not, to be paraded before the press and public without hearing his defence. Ward's case was to become an important exhibit in the long-running argument for disallowing any reporting of committal proceedings, a reform that had been blocked by Henry Brooke but was achieved in 1967 by Labour's Home Secretary, Roy Jenkins.[15]

---

15   The desirability of curtailing publicity became apparent after the saturation coverage of the committal of Dr John Bodkin Adams, charged with euthanising a number of elderly patients, some of whom were not made the subject of counts at his trial. The *Tucker Committee on Proceedings before Examining Justice* Cmnd 479 (1958) found that unrestrained reporting of committal evidence was prejudicial.

In Ward's case, the unfairness was manifest, because the committal included three obnoxious charges that were never levelled against him at his trial – that he had 'conspired with others to keep a brothel at 17 Wimpole Mews, W1, against the peace of our Sovereign Lady the Queen, her Crown and Dignity', and two charges of procuring abortions. Ward's jurors, at his trial which took place less than three weeks later, would have remembered the much-publicised abortion allegations,[16] although they should never have been brought. The jurors would certainly remember, from the saturation press coverage, that the Crown was alleging that Ward kept brothels and procured abortions – prejudice that a few weeks could not possibly dispel.

The proceedings were begun by Mervyn Griffith-Jones, the senior Treasury Counsel, head of a privileged group of barristers with an office in the Old Bailey, and who had a monopoly on prosecuting the most serious criminal trials. It was most extraordinary for him ever to appear for a preliminary hearing, but this was an extraordinary matter. His case was that from June 1961, when Ward leased the flat at 17 Wimpole Mews which he shared with Keeler until February 1962, and again from September to December 1962

---

16   Crawford, *The Profumo Affair*, p. 106.

when it was shared with Mandy Rice-Davies, Ward lived in part on their earnings as prostitutes. There were two charges, of procuration of 'respectable girls' to have intercourse with other men, which would in due course be rejected by the jury at the trial.

In the magistrates' court, Griffith-Jones put his case on Counts 1 and 2 in this nutshell: 'Keeler had frequent intercourse at the flat with a number of men for payment and paid part of the money she received in this way to Ward'. Hence he was living, 'wholly or in part' (i.e. 'in part') on her immoral earnings. But important evidence at the committal – which went entirely unreported – came from an estate agent, who said that Ward rented the Wimpole Mews flat for £21 per week. He had charged Christine nothing and Mandy £6, and allowed them use of the telephone and the heating and the food in the kitchen. Previous prosecutions of landlords who lived off immoral earnings had relied on *excessive* rent as evidence that they knew, and took advantage, of the fact their tenants were prostitutes. Here, the truth was that the tenants, whether prostitutes or not, had lived on Ward.

Keeler began her evidence by swearing – and this is generally accepted as the truth – that she never had intercourse with Ward: 'we were like brother and sister'. Why had she introduced girls to Ward while she was living at Wimpole Mews? 'Because he likes girls.' She had introduced him to five or six models, but what happened afterwards 'depended on the girl' – sometimes, they stayed the night, sometimes they did not. As for the sex she had at Wimpole Mews, 'I had one boyfriend at the time.' She claimed she had vodka-fuelled intercourse once with Ivanov (this questionable claim stood up her £23,000 *News of the World* story about 'The spy who loved me'), and a number of times with Profumo, who once gave her money as a present for her mother. She had received money on a few occasions from a businessman named Eynan who was 'purely a friend'. A man named 'Charles' had given her £50. What part of the money she received had she given to Ward? 'I was not paying the rent at the time and I used to give him more than half,' she replied elliptically. 'I really didn't know what I did with the money. I owed Dr Ward money and paid him what I owed him. I used to borrow money from Dr Ward as spending money.'

Keeler denied she was a prostitute or call girl – 'it was not quite so wrong, once or twice sleeping with a man for money, a man whom I knew well and liked.' Importantly, she denied that Ward had ever been at home at Wimpole Mews when she had sex. But she insisted, in terms coined (so the defence established) by her ghost writer, that 'he had full control of my mind' because she admired him. Her client Mr Eynan was called. He said he had visited Keeler 'three or four times' for sex at the flat, had taken her out to restaurants ('she was an attractive and amusing companion') and lent her money. After sex he would leave £10 or £15, which had not been bargained beforehand. There was never anyone else at the flat. This was the only evidence on Count 1.

Marilyn (Mandy) Rice-Davies deposed to the facts upon which Count 2 was based. Griffith-Jones was adamant that he did not want her to name her clients. When the witness blurted out that 'while I was living at the flat I had intercourse with Lord Astor', she was reprimanded and the clerk taking down her evidence did not record his name. It came up, however, in the most disastrous question that has ever been asked in cross-examination:

> Burge (defence counsel): Do you know that Lord Astor has made a statement to the police saying your allegations are absolutely untrue?
> Rice-Davies (with giggle): He would, wouldn't he?

This contribution to English literary usage went immediately into *The Oxford Dictionary of Quotations* but did not go to an issue in the case: Lord Astor was not alleged to have paid for his one-off pleasure. The witness had shown some malice in the past towards Ward (she deeply resented his sarcastic story that she was interested in Rachman's will) and her evidence that he had introduced her to Savundra was potentially damaging. But had she ever paid him any of the money given her by satisfied clients? Her only 'client' in the six weeks she stayed at the mews was the 'Indian doctor' to whom Ward had introduced her and who had paid £15–£25 for sex on a few occasions. Ward had not asked for rent money, or for payback of a loan, but she said that when she had money she would give him 'two or three pounds a time'.

Committal proceedings do not involve extensive cross-examination, because the defence keeps its powder dry for the trial. Most of the questions to Mandy, and to Chief Inspector Herbert, related to the police having her put in prison merely over a dodgy driving licence when she refused to make a statement against Ward. Later, said the defence, Mr Herbert pretended that she had been guilty of larceny for non-payment of the rent for a cheap television set, so that he could have her brought to court to testify against Ward. To ensure she would repeat her statement at the preliminary hearing, he had arrested and remanded her until the very day of Ward's committal.

Immediately after she had given evidence for the prosecution, Herbert informed her that there would be no criminal proceedings – a threat which should not have been made in the first place, as this was purely a civil matter.

Keeler was asked about the two 'procuration' charges, which amounted to no more than helping Ward to meet two women (one was Sally Norie) to whom he had taken a fancy, and with whom he later had affairs that, although consensual, were described by Griffith-Jones as immoral. 'Even a honeymoon would sound obscene in the hands of my learned friend,' commented James Burge, Ward's defence counsel.

Committal proceedings were meant both as an opportunity for the prosecution to test its witnesses and assess which charges would appear as counts on the trial indictment, and as a safeguard for defendants, who could ask the magistrate to withdraw the charges if there was no evidence to support them. In Ward's case, the charges of which he was eventually convicted related to living on the earnings of prostitution. This offence had been subject to authoritative study in the Wolfenden Report (better known now for its recommendation to decriminalise homosexuality), which explained: 'Prostitution in itself is not, in this country, an offence against the criminal law … it is not illegal for a woman to offer her body to indiscriminate lewdness for hire ... private immorality should not be the concern of the criminal law.'[17]

However, 'for a male person knowingly to live wholly or in part on the earnings of prostitution' *was* a crime, under Section 30 of the Sexual Offences Act, Wolfenden reported, 'based on the desire to protect the prostitute from coercion or exploitation.'[18] It consists, said the report, 'of an arrangement by which a man lives with a prostitute and is wholly or mainly kept by her. Such a man in commonly known as a ponce or *souteneur*'.[19]

It is important to note that Wolfenden regarded the offence as turning on whether the defendant was living wholly or *mainly* on the prostitute's earnings – which was obviously Parliament's intention when the phrase 'wholly or in part' was used in Section 30 of the Sexual Offences Act (1956). In order to have Ward convicted, the judge would in due course instruct the jury that 'in part' could mean merely a *fractional* part – a few pounds, apparently, would suffice. As Ward was earning £4,000 from his practice and £1,500 from portraiture commissions, and both Keeler and

---

17   *Report of the Committee on Homosexual Offences and Prostitution (Wolfenden Report)*, Cmnd 247 (1957) p. 79 para 224.
18   Ibid., p. 100 para 304.
19   Ibid., p. 99 para 301.

Rice-Davies had said that they merely made contributions to household expenses and paid back loans to Ward (not necessarily from their rewards for sexual services) when they could afford to do so, the charges relating to them should not have been committed for trial.

There was a third 'immoral earnings' charge, featuring a real prostitute, Ronna Ricardo, who told the court she had been paid for sex on a number of occasions at Wimpole Mews. She was, dramatically and courageously, to withdraw this evidence at the trial, explaining that police had forced her to give it by threatening to take her baby into care. The jury, unsurprisingly, were to acquit.

The fourth and fifth charges laid on the indictment were of procuration. Section 23 of the 1956 Act made it an offence 'to procure a girl under twenty-one to have unlawful sexual intercourse in any part of the world with a third person'. The law required proof that the defendant had used some pressure or persuasion to overbear the free will of the young woman.[20] The only evidence came from Sally Norie (Count 4) who had been introduced to Ward by Keeler, had been taken out (she was with him at the Cliveden weekend)

20   R v. *Christian* [1913] 78 JP 112.

and had eventually decided of her own free will to sleep with him. The fifth count featured a young Austrian shop assistant who told much the same story – introduced by Keeler, dating Ward, having sex with him for a while and parting on good terms – after an affair that was neither her first nor her last. Neither of these charges should ever have been proceeded with, and it is a poor reflection on the prosecution counsel, the magistrate who approved them, and on the judge who had a duty to withdraw them from the jury because there was no evidence that could sustain them. They were there, improperly, to blacken Ward and help his conviction on Counts 1 and 2: although the jury acquitted on Counts 4 and 5, they were the basis for the prosecution's denigration of him as promiscuous, a thoroughly filthy fellow.

Committal proceedings may have been meant as a safeguard for defendants, to weed out prosecutions based on insufficient evidence, but in this case the magistrate acted as a rubber stamp. He committed Ward for trial on all charges, and marked the uniqueness of the case by sending it to be tried before a High Court judge at the Old Bailey – an unprecedented place for minor sexual offences, which were usually tried before an ordinary circuit judge at Quarter Sessions, the run-of-the-mill crown courts. He did, at least, grant

Ward bail over police objections: this professional man with no previous convictions emerged from the court after twenty-six days in custody, but was given only nineteen days to prepare for his trial. This in itself was gravely unfair – his counsel later requested the Old Bailey judge, Mr Justice 'Archie' Marshall, to postpone it to September, but the application was rejected. There were 'many considerations' which required the trial to start as soon as possible, although the only obvious consideration was political, to bring to an end the scandal attaching to the government over Profumo by finding a scapegoat. The judge did add, almost as an afterthought, that these cosiderations were 'subject of course to justice being done'.[21]

This was the first of many examples of unfair treatment Ward was to receive at the hands of Mr Justice Marshall. Nineteen days was a ridiculously short time to prepare any full-blooded defence to five charges, especially since Ward had been in prison since his arrest and hence unable to gather evidence, and the prosecution was still serving statements from new witnesses (Vicki Barrett's statement came only ten days before the trial itself started). Moreover, as Burge pointed out to the judge, the defence needed

21   Crawford, *The Profumo Affair*, p. 129.

time to locate witnesses who were abroad for the summer. A trial in September would at least have provided a break from the months of media hysteria and sensationalism which had surrounded Profumo's resignation. The *News of the World* had added a quarter of a million readers with its Keeler exclusives and its speculation about upper-class depravity, even forcing Lord Hailsham to declare, 'I am not the man without a head, the man in the iron mask, the man who apparently goes about clad only in a Masonic apron or a visitor to unnamed orgies.'

Moreover, an adjournment was essential to fairness, so jurors could perhaps forget the evidence, inadmissible at the trial, on the abortion charges. This did not actually amount to much – Ward was alleged to have helped, without payment, two women, neither of them his lovers, who needed a termination, one by allowing her to recuperate at Wimpole Mews and the other by helping to fund her operation. When the trial began only nineteen days later, these allegations, never tested, were fresh in peoples' minds. As a matter of interest, many commentators believed – and have stated – that these were dropped. They were not. They were left off the trial indictment, but could have been resurrected for a second trial, had Ward been acquitted, or successful on appeal. The chief clerk at the Old

Bailey was not even sure that the prosecution would not begin with the abortion charges:[22] it decided to keep them in reserve, presumably because the evidence was so weak and the very allegation, made so luridly at the committal, would have worked its poison.

What comes through most vividly, even after a half-century, are the scenes outside the magistrates' court as Keeler, Rice-Davies and the other 'Ward girl' witnesses made their well-dressed entries and exits. It is not uncommon for curious and sometimes angry crowds to gather when persons accused of exceptionally grave crimes, especially against children, arrive at court, usually in a prison van. But these young women were prosecution witnesses, and they were booed and jeered and spat upon, especially by women, who banged on their chauffeured cars with umbrellas. This lynch-mob behaviour, after so many months of moral posturing by politicians and the press, brings to mind Lord Macaulay's warning, as long ago as 1831:

We know of no spectacle so ridiculous as the British public in one of its periodical fits of morality

---

22   See his letter to the editor of the *Criminal Law Review* (October 1963) claiming that the reason why a High Court judge was allocated to try a pimping charge was that he (the clerk of the court) did not know whether the more serious abortion charges would be tried first.

… Once in six or seven years our virtue becomes outrageous. We cannot suffer the laws of religion and decency to be violated. We must make a stand against vice. We must teach libertines that the English people appreciate the importance of domestic ties. Accordingly, some unfortunate man, in no respect more depraved than hundreds whose offences have been treated with lenity, is singled out as an expiatory sacrifice … If he has a profession, he is to be driven from it. He is cut by the higher orders and hissed by the lower. He is, in truth, a sort of whipping-boy, by whose vicarious agonies all the other transgressors of the same class are, it is supposed, sufficiently chastised. We reflect very complacently on our own severity, and compare with great pride the high standard of morals established in England with the Parisian laxity. At length our anger is satiated. Our victim is ruined and heart-broken. And our virtue goes quietly to sleep for seven years more.[23]

That, precisely and presciently, describes the trial of Dr Stephen Ward.

---

23   Lord Macaulay, extract from essay on Thomas Moore's *Letters and Journals of Lord Byron* (1831).

4

THE TRIAL OF STEPHEN WARD

Regina v. *Ward* opened in Court No. 1 of the Old Bailey – hitherto reserved for murderers and traitors and defendants accused of the greatest crimes – on 22 July 1963. The one hundred reserved media seats (half for foreign reporters) were at the back, behind the dock where it was difficult to hear or see. The best seats in the stalls, so to speak, were those reserved for distinguished visitors, with a clear view over the bewigged heads of the barristers towards the judge, jury and the witness box. The VIPs on opening day included Lady Parker, wife of the Chief Justice. That she should have been invited to sit in the box seat of a trial over any appeal from which her husband would preside, in order to watch the performance of a witness whose behaviour in the *Gordon* case was already the subject of an appeal he would have to decide the following week, was one of the casual improprieties that nobody cared about in 1963. What Lady Parker told her husband about the star witness of 'the trial of the century' is not known: what he thought of Christine Keeler would soon become an issue in the trial itself.

There were five counts in the indictment. The first accused Ward of living off Keeler's earnings as a prostitute at Wimpole Mews between June 1961 and (effectively) February 1962, and the second referred to the earnings there of Marilyn Rice-Davies, who had moved into the mews after a quarrel with Rachman (who had been 'keeping' her in a nearby flat) in October 1962 and remained until the shooting incident with Edgecombe in mid-December. Griffith-Jones explained that the prosecution case was that both were prostitutes, loosely defined as 'women who sold their bodies for money': the prosecution had to prove beyond reasonable doubt that they were, and that Ward was habitually in their company – then the burden would shift to Ward to prove, albeit on the balance of probabilities, that he was not living on their immoral earnings either in whole or in part. The prosecution accepted that, if they *were* prostitutes, their evidence would require 'corroboration' – a word that juries even today find difficult to understand, but which simply means confirmation from an independent witness.

Keeler Testifies

The prosecution evidence on Count 1 was provided by Keeler herself, although at an early stage in it she plaintively asserted, 'I am not a prostitute and never have been.' So how had she obtained money in this period? She named a benefactor with whom she had not had sex and a Mr Eynan with whom she had, although Ward was never in the flat on the half-dozen occasions when she had indulged him and had never arranged their meetings. Then there was Profumo, who had on one occasion given her money ('a little something for your mother'), again in Ward's absence, and Ivanov (once) after giving her vodka but nothing more. Apart from Edgecombe and Gordon and an occasional boyfriend (they were irrelevant because they had not paid) the only other man from whom she had received money as the result of sex was named 'Charles' (she said she had forgotten his second name – it was multimillionaire property developer Charles Clore). She said that Ward had introduced them, and had later said that if she visited him in Mayfair he would give her money. She visited him, and after intercourse he gave her £50. (Under cross-examination, she made clear that Ward did not ask her to go for his sake, but 'suggested I could get some money from Charles because I was hard up'.)[24] What did she do with that money? 'I repaid a loan with some of it, to Dr Ward.' Did she give any of the money from Eynan and Profumo and Charles to Ward? 'Well, yes, to pay my debts.' What proportion? 'Well, I usually owed him more than I ever made: I only gave him half of that.'[25]

This was the only evidence the prosecution elicited from her on Count 1, and Keeler agreed with defence counsel that she had been allowed to live rent-free at Wimpole Mews and had use of telephone, electricity and hot water and that she earned money from modelling. Given that she had borrowed money from Ward, could he be convicted if she paid him back from 'immoral' earnings? Could he be convicted of living off or *on* her? The only other prosecution witness was Mr Eynan.[26] He said he had not been introduced to her by Ward and that a sexual relationship with her began before she moved to the mews, where they only had intercourse three or four times, in the middle of the day when it was known that Ward would be at his surgery. He had taken her to restaurants and entertainment, and she was an amusing and

24   Ludovic Kennedy, *The Trial of Stephen Ward* (Penguin, 1963) p. 50.
25   Ibid., pp. 40–42.
26   Ibid., p. 95.

attractive companion. He had only met Ward once, as he was leaving the flat. Mr Eynan was called as a prosecution witness, but why was he not joined by Profumo since the Crown was relying on the latter's £20 gift as evidence against Ward? At this point, the political, or at least class, bias became clear. James Eynan was a nondescript businessman who could be held up to public obloquy. Profumo, however, had to be protected. He had suffered enough for his sins, and the public could not be vouchsafed the spectacle of him appearing, all pinstriped, in the witness box confessing his sexual indiscretions. The multimillionaire property developer Charles Clore should in fairness to the defence also have been called, since his name had probably emerged in the course of the investigation. If it had, police should have taken a statement from him, and the prosecutors should have called him as a witness. Similarly with Dr Savundra. If wealth brought these men their exemption then the trial will appear even more of a travesty. The answer is likely to be found in the prosecution papers which the National Archives refuses to release, perhaps because the answer will be found within them.

Did Ward know Keeler was having sex in the flat and repaying his loans with some of the proceeds? In his evidence, he emphatically denied it. He knew Profumo was visiting and had 'a pretty shrewd idea' that they were having sex, but knew nothing of the gift of money for her mother. As for Eynan, 'I did not know of the relationship or the fact that he was giving her money.' That left standing only the mysterious Charles:

> Griffith-Jones: Miss Keeler has told us that on one occasion she did go round to see the man Charles (i.e. at your instigation).
>
> Ward: No Sir. I would never suggest such a thing. That was quite wrong. She is lying.
>
> GJ: Complete fabrication by that girl?
>
> Ward: Complete fabrication.
>
> GJ: Did you tell her in effect that it was alright to go with men for money?
>
> Ward: (shouting) NO SIR I DID NOT. I did not know of the relationship with Eynan or the fact that he was giving her money.
>
> GJ: Don't you think that the control of a man aged fifty over a girl of eighteen in an atmosphere of immorality such as must have been the atmosphere in Wimpole Mews...
>
> Ward: (passionately) That was *not* the atmosphere in Wimpole Mews. You have described a relationship which went on over a long time. Most of the time in Wimpole Mews I was playing bridge or drawing. You have concentrated all these incidents

into a short time which gives a false picture, and I am not that sort of person at all.[27]

'Lucky' Gordon: Keeler Lies Again

Since there was no evidence that Ward was aware of Profumo's gifts or Eynan's payments, the crucial evidence related to 'Charles' – the occasion when, so Keeler alleged, Ward had sent her to a man who lived just off Park Lane to obtain money for sex so she could pay off her debts, including her debts to him. Was she lying? To convict, the jury must have believed her evidence, although they could hardly have done so, or entertained no reasonable doubt about her honesty, had they known she lied on oath at a trial only six weeks previously. That is why this part of her cross-examination becomes very important:

Burge: Did you take the oath on a previous occasion when you attended the trial of a man called Gordon?
Keeler: Yes.
Burge: Did you tell the whole truth then?
Keeler: Yes, I did.
Burge: Did you say all your injuries were caused by Gordon?

---

27   Ibid., pp. 164–5.

Keeler: Yes, and they were.

Burge: Did you know that the man Gordon alleged that the injuries were not caused by him?

Keeler: The man is mad. Of course they were.

Burge: And that he wished to call two witnesses, one called Fenton and a man called Comacchio?

Keeler: Yes.

Burge: And did you say those two men were not present at the time of the incident?

Keeler: Yes, I said they were not present because they were not present.

Burge: Did you know that Sergeant Burrows, the officer in this case, was the officer in that case as well?

Keeler: Yes.

Keeler had lied then, to put a man in prison for three years, and now she was unashamedly maintaining that lie. The jury could not convict Ward on the evidence of a perjurer. The prosecution, if it knew there was evidence that proved her guilty (the tape recording, the statement of Fenton and Comacchio that Gordon never laid a finger on her, and a statement by John Hamilton-Marshall admitting that it was he who had given her the black eye) had a duty to make this known to the defence. Indeed, they should not have put her in the box as a witness of truth. Did

Griffith-Jones know about this evidence? It is hard to believe that he did not, because of the startling fact that Sergeant Burrows, the officer in the *Ward* case, was sitting in front of him in court. Burrows was the officer in the *Gordon* case as well, who had taken the statements and seized the tape that proved Keeler a liar. Presumably he told his counsel, Griffith-Jones, about the fresh evidence in the *Gordon* appeal, which by 22 July had been filed and was set down for hearing on 30 July. The Director of Public Prosecutions had it as well – did he not ensure that it was passed to the Ward defence? The three Court of Appeal judges had carefully scrutinised the lengthy transcript (the interview with Keeler lasted ten hours) and they had edited it so only references to her lies against Gordon were extracted. They knew that it contained material highly relevant to Ward's defence and, as we shall see, they acted to ensure that it was not disclosed.

Was this crucial evidence withheld from Ward's defence, and if so, why? Why did the Court of Appeal hear the *Gordon* case at the end of Ward's trial, and not before it? As we shall see from the final speeches and summing-up, and the behaviour of the Court of Appeal, this is a matter of scandal and concern and will remain so until fully investigated and honestly explained.

Count 2 – Rice-Davies Testifies

The evidence on Count 2 was provided by Mandy Rice-Davies. She only lived in the mews for six weeks, having gone there after a quarrel with Rachman, who had 'kept' her in a flat, with jewels and furs and an allowance of £80 per week. She still loved him and hoped to marry him, so she said, and was so upset when he died suddenly in November that she attempted suicide. Ward permitted her parents, who came down from Birmingham, to stay in the mews for a week to look after her when she returned from hospital. She admitted a degree of malice towards him at the time of the police interview, both because he had made cynical comments to her parents that her reason for the suicide attempt was disappointment that Rachman had not made a will in her favour and because Ward later acquired a lease on the flat in which she had been 'kept' by Rachman (she was sentimental about it and wanted the lease herself). Her evidence, however, was clear that although she had sex with a boyfriend while she stayed at the flat, and once with Lord Astor, who had pounced on her behind Ward's back, neither had paid her. When Ward was behind with the rent he had asked her to borrow £250 from a man named Ropner, but she did not fancy him and did not go to bed with him and did not ask him for money. (Ward was particularly indignant about this evidence – he said that Ropner was an old friend and if he had needed money, he would have asked Ropner for it himself.)

The only allegation Rice-Davies made that could possibly sustain a conviction on Count 2 concerned a man referred to as 'the Indian doctor', who was in fact the Ceylonese businessman Dr Savundra. She and Ward had met him in a coffee bar in Marylebone High Street, and the next day he had called at the mews when Ward was out. Later, Ward asked whether she liked him, and when she said she did, Ward explained, 'He is a very rich man and wants to have your room because he has got a girlfriend and it's difficult for him to take her anywhere', and he had already paid £25 in rent. Mandy said that was fine by her – she was often out herself, and did not mind Savundra, whom she rather liked, using it for assignations during the day. But, Rice-Davies continued, Ward had said, 'If you like the doctor, why let his girlfriend go out with him? Why don't you go out with him?' Savundra came round the next day, and Mandy went in with him – into the bedroom, where they had sex about five times over the next two weeks, and he left £15–£25 on the dressing table each time.[28] This

28   Ibid., pp. 66–7.

was the most incriminating evidence in the case, but it was never corroborated. Ward emphatically denied that he knew anything about the Indian doctor's visits to Mandy, although he admitted that Savundra had been brought to see him by a friend after Keeler left, and they had met in a coffee bar to discuss whether he could rent her old room. Savundra issued a press statement denying that he ever had sex with Mandy, although this was not put to her in cross-examination (no doubt to avoid a repetition of 'he would, wouldn't he'). It is not known whether he made a statement to police but they certainly should have interviewed him. He was not called by the prosecution; why not? The mystery of the missing wealthy witnesses – Clore, Profumo, Astor and Savundra – hangs heavy in the history of this case and will not be dispelled until the prosecution papers are permitted to be released.

If Savundra was a paying customer of Mandy's at Wimpole Mews, conviction on Count 2 still required Ward to know of the fact and to know that any payments he received from Mandy were from her earnings for sex work. This was problematic, because she was being charged only £6 per week for rent and she ran up a big telephone bill and she admitted to receiving hand-outs from Ward. She did not volunteer in the witness box the important fact that she was still receiving an £80 weekly allowance from Rachman, which continued even after his death, and that she had received a very large cash hand-out in October from him to induce her to move back and give him another chance to honour his promise that he would leave his wife. 'How much did you give Ward?' the judge asked her. 'In all about £25. I paid for the food as well, you see.' Ward in his evidence said that she paid him about £24 for the first month's rent, plus £5 for use of the telephone, in the course of the six weeks. This would not have covered all the rent, or the expenses of her parents' stay. Given her other sources of income, and the undisclosed allowance and gift from Rachman, the notion that Ward had 'lived on' her earnings from Savundra is unreal. Ward said that he was earning £4,000 from his practice and another £1,500 from his work in portraiture, and although he had no account-ing system and was reckless with and sometimes in need of money, he had no reason to ask for hand-outs from sex work. When asked by Griffith-Jones what he really thought Rice-Davies was doing, he replied with some asperity:

She was in the flat for only a month before she attempted to commit suicide. She had come from a relationship which was an intended marriage

with Rachman and she was not short of money and was well dressed. I provided food in the flat and she had few expenses. She was a pretty girl and she was taken out by people. There wasn't a question of living off her. *If anything she was living off me.*
Griffith-Jones: Even if you know there was one man, what do you think she was doing it for? Pure love, as you say?
Ward: No, not in this particular case. I think it was for enjoyment of the sexual act.

It was the first and only time in this seven-day trial that the notion that a woman might have sex for pleasure, rather than either for love or for money, was canvassed as a possibility.

Rice-Davies admitted that pressure had been placed on her by Inspector Herbert – after she had refused to make a statement against Ward, he had arranged for her to be taken to Holloway Prison in connection with a forged driving licence and had interviewed her there and she did not want to go back. Then he had arrested her for theft of an £82 television that had been rented for her, and she had been released on an unnecessarily high £1,000 bail to return to Marylebone Magistrates' Court on 28 June, which just happened to be the opening day, in that court,

Stephen Ward, artist and lover.

Happy days at the Cliveden pool. Stephen Ward, with Christine (right), Mandy (left) and Paula Hamilton-Marshall (centre).

John and Valerie Profumo attend a dinner party for Princess Margaret.

Ward's sketch of Christine, now exhibited in the National Portrait Gallery.

Eugene Ivanov, the spy who may have loved Christine.

Minister for War no more: John Profumo on the day he resigned.

'Lucky' Gordon, literally framed by police.

Prime Minister Harold Macmillan sets off to explain himself in the great Profumo debate, 17 June 1963.

Behind a glass, darkly: the iconic photograph of Stephen Ward, off to see his barristers.

Make way for Mandy! Police protect her from the crowds at the committal proceedings.

Crowds gather early for the opening day of *R* v. *Ward*: the Old Bailey, 22 July 1963.

Mandy and Christine leaving the Old Bailey at the end of first day's play: 22 July.

Police hold back the angry crowd outside the Old Bailey on 25 July after Ward has testified.

Witnesses for the prosecution, Mandy and Christine.

There but for the grace of God ... James Eynan, Christine's middle-class lover, summonsed outside the Old Bailey. Why were Profumo, Clore, Savundra and Astor never in this picture?

BELOW LEFT Mr Mervyn Griffith-Jones striding early to court on 30 July, the day that began with the Gordon cover-up and ended with Ward's suicide attempt.

BELOW RIGHT 'He would, wouldn't he?' Lord 'Bill' Astor.

Police cordon holds back crowds outside the Old Bailey on 25 July lest they harass the real prostitutes who testified on that day.

'Never glad confident morning again' – Stephen Ward puts on a brave face as he leaves for court on the morning of his suicide, 30 July.

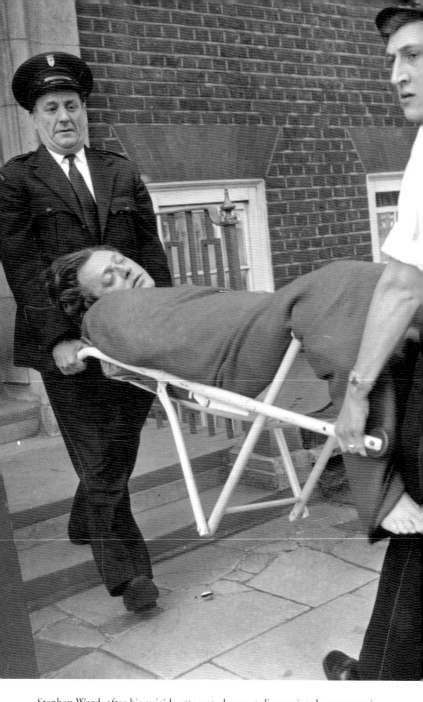

Stephen Ward, after his suicide attempt, does not disappoint the paparazzi.

of Ward's committal. Once she had given evidence for the prosecution, the police dropped their threat to charge her. The defence found her infuriatingly candid, although Burge failed to cross-examine her in a way that would help his client:

Burge: There is something you want very much as a result of this case, don't you?

Mandy: Yes Sir.

Burge: Money?

Mandy: Oh yes.

Burge: Big money?

Mandy: If it's possible, yes.

Burge: The value of your story depends on the conviction of this man.

Mandy: No Sir.

Burge: Don't you realise that because of the laws of libel your story would not have the same value if he was acquitted than if he was convicted?

Mandy: I hope he is acquitted.

(When asked by Griffith-Jones why she hoped for Ward's acquittal, she explained: 'I know what it's like in jail. Why, you might as well arrest every bachelor in London.')[29]

---

29   Ibid., p. 73.

The Other Counts

There was much more in the trial, but the above passages contain the gist of the actual evidence on the conviction counts. The two procuration charges, Counts 4 and 5, should never have been included. Sally Norie had met Ward and Keeler when lunching with her boyfriend: Keeler had attracted the boyfriend while Ward had made a play for Sally, who in turn played hard to get over several meetings and visits to Cliveden (she had been there on the Profumo weekend) and she resisted until she knew and liked him well enough to have sex – which was free and voluntary and (presumably, although it could not be mentioned) enjoyable. She had affairs before and since, but not with any of his friends. There was no element of 'procuration', and the judge should not have left this count to the jury – it was 'Archie' Marshall's duty to protect a defendant from the danger of conviction on insufficient evidence. It was a duty that he failed to do in respect of Stephen Ward. Similarly with Count 5, in which an Austrian woman (she was given anonymity, because Griffith-Jones said she came from a 'good family')[30] who worked in a shop which Keeler frequented had been asked by Keeler to go on a date with Ward. They went out to lunch a few times, and

---

30   Ibid., p. 55.

then to Cliveden, where she slept with him. Why? Because, she said under cross-examination, she liked him and he liked her. The only basis upon which these consenting adult sexual encounters could be put before the jury as a crime of 'procuration' was that Keeler had been Ward's agent in effecting the intro- duction – but as the sex was consensual and no money passed, the acquittal was inevitable. The charges were on the indictment to introduce evidence about Ward's bad reputation as a serial seducer of 'respectable' young women. They also gave an important tactical advantage to the prosecution: the jury could acquit and feel fair, even if they convicted on other counts.

Count 3, however, was a different matter. Here, Ward was accused of living off the earnings of real prosti- tutes, and although the jury acquitted, the perjured evidence must have left its mark. It featured two women, Vicki Barrett and Ronna Ricardo, the former as inventive as the latter was courageous. Ricardo had, at the magistrates' court, testified about two-way mirrors and meeting men for money at Ward's flat. Afterwards, however, she had gone to Scotland Yard and admitted it was mostly lies – she had been threat- ened by Inspector Herbert with having her baby taken into care and her sister taken to a remand home unless she signed a statement against Ward, but she could not face lying under oath at the Old Bailey. 'Mr Herbert told me they would take my baby if I didn't make the statements.' For seasoned court reporters, her evidence had the ring of truth, even after the prosecutor, who had her declared a 'hostile witness', finished cross-examining her. The judge, whose threats to punish her unless she reverted to the obviously false story she had told at the magistrates' court were disgraceful (and revealed his real bias), intervened to say, 'I shall have to tell the jury completely to disregard this witness.'[31] This, as we shall see, was a misdirection. A hostile witness who goes back on her deposition cannot be relied upon in relation to the facts in either of her statements – they cancel each other out. But the jury can take cognisance of the reasons she gives for her tergiversation, and the improper and cruel pressure put on her by police in relation to her baby and her young sister would, if accepted, provide powerful support for the defence case that improper police pressure had been put on Mandy Rice-Davies as well, by a police inspector out to get results.

Vicki Barrett was a long-standing streetwalker who had been brought on prostitution charges to Marylebone Magistrates' Court on the very day of Ward's committal. She was soon having herself photographed (for sale to tabloids) and telling a story

---

31   Crawford, *The Profumo Affair*, p. 144.

which seemed just too good for the prosecution to be true. She maintained that over several months in early 1963 she had been picked up by Ward in his Jaguar and taken to the mews, where a naked man would be lying face down on the bed, his buttocks presumably twitching, awaiting a caning or horsewhipping which she would administer, having quickly changed into high heels, black stockings and suspender belt. Ward would supply her with a condom as she entered (a streetwalker without her own supply?), make coffee while she whacked at £1 a stroke, and keep the money in order to save it up for her to buy a flat (although he never gave it to her and, incredibly, she never asked for it). It was a preposterous story, especially as these events were alleged to have taken place at a time when Ward's house was under police surveillance. Her evidence was served on the defence only ten days before the trial started, and Ward's lawyers made a considerable – and successful – effort to find witnesses to disprove it. Barrett's sensational story was not, in the end, accepted by the jury, but it did cast a sordid pallor over the defendant, who had hired (and sketched) her on one occasion. It also took up defence time and resources which would have been better spent on refuting stories about 'Charles' and 'the Indian doctor'. (A reporter, who brought Barrett the news of Ward's death, heard her spontaneous tear-stained confession, 'It was all lies – it was not true I went with other men', but she refused his request to go to the police to retract her Old Bailey evidence.[32])

The handful of brief defence witnesses included a prostitute who worked with Barrett and refuted her testimony and Noel Howard-Jones, the brave young law student who gave Ward sanctuary in his flat during the trial. His 'character' evidence testifying to Ward's kindness and the usually sedate atmosphere of the mews, with bridge parties rather than orgies, earned him a nasty but discrediting cross-examination about his brief fling with Christine. Ward had mentioned in his evidence his assistance to the security services, but 'Mr Woods' did not appear – MI5 did not respond to the frantic attempt by Ward's solicitor to track him down. The prosecutor dismissed Ward's claim about his connection with MI5 and the jury must have regarded it as a fantasy. Or, they may have thought, as the judge was to suggest they could think, that lack of confirmation simply proved that Ward was lying.

The Gordon Appeal

After the evidence, the trial moved on to final speeches and the judge's summing-up. This stage was reached

---

32   Kennedy, *The Trial of Stephen Ward*, pp. 228–31.

on Monday 29 July, and it fell to James Burge, on behalf of Ward, to make the first closing address. It is no longer the case that the prosecutor has the last word to the jury, but that was the procedure in 1963. James Burge was not a Queen's Counsel, of equivalent ranking to the senior Treasury Counsel who would follow him, and never become one – according to rumour, precisely because he had fearlessly defended Stephen Ward. (For this reason, he later became one of John Mortimer's role-models for 'Rumpole of the Bailey', the barrister who is never promoted because he gets up judicial noses.) Ward had liked him, and made the mistake of retaining him for a trial that required a leader like Gerald Gardiner QC or Jeremy Hutchinson QC, who had faced down Griffith-Jones so effectively in the *Lady Chatterley* trial three years before.

Observers like Ludovic Kennedy noted that Burge was repeatedly humiliated in front of the jury by the judge (who affected not to remember his name), and a juror who spoke to Knightley and Kennedy thought that he was outclassed – he never captured, or undermined, the moral high ground held by the prosecutor. He lacked finesse, and made a few forensic blunders, but his performance was not so inadequate as to serve as a ground of appeal. He cross-examined the police most effectively over the improper pressure they had brought to bear on witnesses (particularly Rice-Davies), although in this respect his efforts were undermined by a judge who could believe no ill of metropolitan police inspectors (as a matter of interest, Chief Inspector Herbert was discovered, after his death in 1966, to have a secret slush fund (of about £0.5m in today's money) redolent of corruption, and was then the subject of a Scotland Yard internal corruption inquiry that has never been published). Burge's difficult job in court had been made more difficult by a highly strung and highly strained client who, when he was not sketching the witness and the lawyers, was distracting his counsel by sending a stream of notes from the dock.

However, there is force in the criticism that his final speech was lopsided. He made a bitter, electrifying and utterly justified attack on the two procuration charges, which had 'not a vestige of truth', but then concentrated on demolishing Count 3 – based on the 'immoral earnings' evidence of Ricardo and Barrett. This was hardly necessary, as Ricardo had self-destructed and defence witnesses had been called to refute Barrett, which they had done quite effectively. This tactical dilemma was caused by the prosecutor's last-minute decision to put Barrett on the stand. It meant that most defence fire was concentrated on her sensational stories about paid whippings at the mews, and there was little other than Ward's own evidence to counter Keeler's testimony about 'Charles' and Profumo and James Eynan on Count 1, and Mandy's recollections of 'the Indian doctor' on Count 2. Mandy, in evidence, expressed the hope that Ward would be acquitted but this, as Ward himself said, was 'the kiss of death'. The crowds outside the Old Bailey had been booing and hissing an 18-year-old woman whom they viewed as an unapologetic hussy, and their prejudices must have affected the jurors. The fact that she seemed on Ward's side while giving evidence against him made that evidence seem all the more credible, notwithstanding the oppressive way it had been obtained by the police.

Burge summarised the issue on Counts 1 and 2 reasonably enough, by asking, 'Was this life of Ward's led for fun or profit?' Was he living as a parasite on the earnings of prostitution, or was he merely 'a man with an artistic temperament and high sexual proclivities, leading a dissolute life.' The defence had, from the outset (and mistakenly, even in the climate of 1963), gone along with the prosecution contention that Ward was 'utterly immoral' – by virtue of the fact that he had sex with a number of girlfriends and occasionally frequented prostitutes. Burge warned them that the girls' evidence would require 'corroboration' although they may not have understood what that meant and they later obtained no help from the judge.

The defence final speech began at 11 a.m. on Monday 29 July and took three and a half hours. On Tuesday, the 'Lucky' Gordon appeal was due to be heard by the Court of Criminal Appeal, sitting in the High Court at the other end of Fleet Street.[33] Quite why Gordon's appeal was listed at the end of the Ward trial rather than before it is unclear. All the judges had read the tape transcript and the witness statements and knew that this was material that might be of help to Ward. It is not clear why the evidence for Keeler's perjury, collected by one of the police officers who were also in the *Ward* case, was not disclosed to Ward's defence. This non-disclosure would, today, be grounds to quash the conviction.

Burge had to say something to the jury at the end of his speech on Monday about how they should receive next day's news of the Gordon appeal, although of course he could not be certain it would be upheld. He had 'laid the ground' by asking Keeler questions about her evidence in that case, and she had repeated the lies under oath. But the evidence for her perjury was in statements and a tape recording in the possession of the

---

33   It later, in 1966, became the Court of Appeal (Criminal Division).

Lord Chief Justice's clerk. So all that Burge could say to the jury was that the appeal was pending, there was an allegation of perjury and, 'If that conviction against "Lucky" Gordon had been quashed, and if the allegation was correct that she had given perjured evidence, think of the assistance it would have been to the defence.'

What the jury actually thought, as a result of that comment, made to them before lunch on Monday, is difficult to guess, but it did alert them to the imminent Court of Appeal decision and to the fact that if Gordon's conviction was quashed on fresh evidence that showed Keeler had committed perjury, this would assist the defence. It was the best that Burge could do, handicapped by lack of knowledge about what the Chief Justice was planning, and having no opportunity to address the jury again.

The closing speech for the prosecution began at 3.30 p.m. on Monday. Mr Griffith-Jones told them, repeatedly, that Ward was 'a filthy fellow' and 'a thoroughly immoral man' which was 'highly relevant in this case'. He provided a definition of a prostitute, 'a woman who offers her body for sexual intercourse or lewd acts for money'[34] (this was an error – a prostitute must be indiscriminate or arbitrary in offering

---

34   Crawford, *The Profumo Affair*, p. 160.

her favours). He submitted that both Mandy and Christine 'were prepared to go to bed with any man – certainly a good number of men – for money … they are, in the eyes of the law, prostitutes'.

At this point, Monday's proceedings stood adjourned until the usual time of 10.30 a.m. on Tuesday. At 9 a.m. on Tuesday (an hour when courts in Britain hardly ever sit), and without notice to the press, Lord Chief Justice Parker, together with Justice Sachs and Justice Widgery (later Chief Justice Widgery), heard 'Lucky' Gordon's appeal. The Chief Justice's court was, notwithstanding the lack of notice, packed with journalists, who were treated to nine minutes of pre-planned judicial cover-up. Gordon's counsel had scarcely opened his mouth when Parker jumped in to ask whether he had read the new witness statements and whether he would be apply-ing to call those witnesses at an appeal. 'That would be my application,' confirmed the barrister. Parker, as if his worst fear had been realised, then turned to the prosecution counsel. 'We have read with care the further statements … if this evidence had been before the jury they might have felt there was reasonable doubt?' Counsel for the prosecution agreed (he would wouldn't he?) with the Chief Justice: 'I am bound to agree … I feel that I cannot argue effectively to the contrary.' In what continued as a short colloquy with barristers who grovelled in agreement, the Chief Justice went on, 'for obvious reasons it is inadvisable that the person from whom these statements have been obtained should give evidence here'. It was far from obvious to anyone else in court, since hearing the witnesses would at least explain why Gordon's conviction was being quashed. Parker went on, as the barristers on both sides nodded their bewigged heads in respectful obeisance to their Chief Justice.

> It may well be that the complainant's [i.e. Keeler's] evidence was completely truthful … I would like to make it clear once more that the court is not holding that the complainant's evidence is untruthful. She may well have been speaking the truth, but at the same time this further evidence might have raised a doubt in the jury's mind.

There was no 'judgment' as such – the Chief Justice simply announced that Gordon's conviction was quashed, and directed that a copy of his remarks in open court should be transcribed and rushed by special messenger to the Old Bailey, where (as we shall see) they were used by prosecutor and judge to bolster Keeler's credibility – quite incredibly, given that this decision had been based on sworn evidence by three witnesses, and a taped self-confession that she had lied. The original of the ten-hour tape with the confession was vital evidence in the *Ward* case, and the court should have ordered that it be held by the police and copies of the transcript supplied to both parties in Ward's trial. Instead, Parker ordered that a police officer 'deliver the tape out of the custody of the court to the person from whom it was obtained': i.e. Robin Durie, Keeler's manager, who had tried to keep it secret all along.

Keeler's lawyer suddenly stood up to provide one last *Alice in Wonderland* moment:

> Mr Solomon: My Lord, may I with very great respect make an application in respect of the tape on behalf of Miss Keeler?
>
> The Lord Chief Justice: You have got no standing here.
>
> Mr Solomon: I know. That is why I said with very great respect.
>
> The Lord Chief Justice: Then we cannot listen to you, I am sorry.[35]

At this point, the session came to its bathetic close.

And so this infamous – or 'unfortunate' as Lord Parker later described it – appeal ended, after just nine

---

35   Original transcript of *Gordon* Appeal. Viewed in National Archives.

minutes. The Lord Chief Justice had managed to time it, and dispose of it, so as – quite deliberately – to hide the evidence upon which the court was upholding the appeal, despite the fact (or because of it) that the evidence was highly relevant to Stephen Ward's innocence of a charge on which he was being tried at the Old Bailey. Because judges – and lawyers – did not at the time care very much about 'criminal justice' or realise that miscarriages occur when evidence is covered up, there was no immediate concern about this aspect of Parker's behaviour. But the academic experts at the *Criminal Law Review* did point out four fundamental errors these three judges made in what I have to suggest was the rush to have Stephen Ward unjustly convicted:

1. The court actually had no power to quash an appeal on the basis of fresh evidence unless it actually *heard* that evidence. It could not rely on witness statements unless the witnesses confirmed them at a hearing in court, and it could not be relieved of that duty by a prosecution that colluded in not wanting the evidence to be made public.

2. There was no 'judgment' as such and no reasons given for the decision to overturn the conviction other than a reference to hidden evidence. This was a breach of the 'open justice' principle, i.e. that justice must be seen to be done. The very basis of this principle

– Bentham's explanation, previously referred to, that 'publicity is the very soul of justice. It keeps the judge, while trying, under trial,' – was turned on its head. The public could not judge the adequacy and propriety of the judicial behaviour that had overturned the result of a three-day criminal trial.

3. The 'obvious reasons' for secrecy were not obvious at all. It might be assumed that Parker was referring to the ongoing trial of Ward, in which case he should have said so – his lack of frankness added to the atmosphere of furtive manipulation. Once Ward's trial was identified as the reason, of course, the court might have been hard put to explain why it was not testing, or at least sending to the Old Bailey for possible testing, evidence that was highly relevant to Ward's defence.

4. The most serious aspect of the *Gordon* appeal, the *Criminal Law Review* was emboldened to say, was that the court had brought upon itself 'the suspicion of yielding to external pressures in a case linked with a major public and political scandal' which would lead to loss of public confidence in the judiciary.[36] There was a suspicion, among barristers at the time, that Parker and Widgery and Marshall were willing tools of a government that wanted Ward condemned – in prison

---

36   *Criminal Law Review*, September 1963, pp. 602–3.

he would be out of sight and therefore out of mind. But this is simplistic. These judges were operating at a time when they thought themselves (and, to be fair, others thought of them) as custodians of public morality. Ward had become not a human sacrifice on the altar of family life, but a test case of the acceptability of an alternative lifestyle. If a test case goes wrong, the defendant and his cause is triumphant. (All these judges had in mind the recent test case over *Lady Chatterley's Lover*, which Griffith-Jones had lost with the consequence that three million copies of a book about the pleasures of sex outside marriage were eagerly consumed by the public.) This time, virtue should triumph, and these judges were prepared to bend the rules, to behave improperly, to ensure that it would. It was, as Griffith-Jones came to put it in his final appeal to the jury, *in the national interest* that Ward should be convicted.

This was an era when, as one eminent law lord put it, 'The Old Bailey is hardly the SW3 of the legal profession' – judges were culled from commercial or property practices, and no one talked of 'human rights' or even of civil liberties (the first book on that subject, Henry Street's *Freedom, the Individual and the Law*, was published later in the year). Yet the Chief Justice must have followed the *Ward* case because of its saturation coverage – his wife, after all, had witnessed the first day – and would have known that Christine Keeler was the prosecution's most vital witness. The judges had read the evidence – the tape transcript and the witness statements signed under threat of prison if they proved false – and they must have realised that the impact was not merely to 'raise a doubt in the jury's mind' but to establish (on her own confession, and three compelling witness statements) that Keeler had given perjured evidence. It was obvious that the Ward trial would not be fair unless the defence was given the opportunity to call this evidence before the jury. That was what the interests of justice required. Ward's junior counsel, who later became a fine prosecutor and a distinguished high court judge, described the conduct of the Court of Appeal as 'reprehensible' (Appendix A) because it actually undermined the point about Keeler that was being made by the defence. Lord Parker ordered that his deliberately equivocal remarks be transcribed, typed up and taken by special courier (who ran down Fleet Street and up Ludgate Hill) to Justice Marshall and Mr Griffith-Jones. At the Old Bailey it enabled the latter to break into the ending of his final speech for the prosecution, with the approval of the judge, and deliver from counsel's bench the following announcement:

Gordon's appeal has been allowed. That does not mean to say that the Court of Criminal Appeal have found that Miss Keeler is lying. As I understand from the note I have, the Lord Chief Justice said that it might be that Miss Keeler's evidence was completely truthful, but in view of the fact that there were witnesses now available who were not available at the trial, it was felt that the court could not necessarily say that the jury in that case would have returned the same verdict as they did if those two witnesses had been called.

That is all it amounts to. The Court of Criminal Appeal have not found whether Miss Keeler was telling the truth: they have allowed the appeal simply and solely because these two witnesses were not there.

This was highly irregular. Counsel must not themselves give evidence, and Griffith-Jones's statement that the only reason why the appeal was allowed was because two witnesses had not attended was simply untrue. The appeal was allowed because there was evidence from a number of witnesses, and a tape recording, from which a jury could conclude that she had lied. But Griffith-Jones went on, in a comment that should ensure that the *Ward* case now goes to the Court of Appeal and that his conviction is overturned:

Finally, if you convict in this case and should there be anything in the Gordon case of which you do not know which has turned up in this appeal, it will afford this defendant a ground of appeal thereafter to the same Court which has decided the Gordon appeal this morning, and that Court will be in possession of all the facts, so that no injustice, you may think, can have been done.[37]

This notion that they need not worry because there is a court of appeal that can put everything right is an unacceptable way of soothing a jury's conscience about bringing in a conviction where they are not in fact sure beyond reasonable doubt – there is a court of appeal, certainly, but as the record of the CCRC shows, it does *not* always put jury verdict's right. While it is acceptable for judges to tell juries 'you must take the law from me – if I am wrong the Court of Appeal can correct me', this must never be said in relation to factual issues to encourage a jury to convict, because it is not true. It must not be said by judges, or by prosecuting counsel, in whose mouth it counts as improper advocacy. In defence of Griffith-Jones it may be said that it was an 'off-the-cuff' comment about a note

---

37   Crawford, *The Profumo Affair*, p. 163.

that had just been handed up to him. But that made it all the more important for Justice Marshall to take action to correct the appallingly unfair situation that had arisen. He should, of course, have insisted that the defence be shown the statements collected by the very police who were sitting in front of him in court during the trial and re-open the evidence so the jury could, if the defence wished, call these witnesses to show Keeler as a perjurer. He did nothing. Indeed, as we shall soon see, he did worse than nothing. He endorsed Griffith-Jones's comments by re-reading Lord Parker's disingenuous statement, and directed the jury to 'exclude from your minds' any question about the veracity of Keeler's evidence in the *Gordon* case which had been an important defence point. As Ludovic Kennedy, who was there, comments, 'If the Ward jury had known that Christine had lied on oath in the witness box, not only at Gordon's trial but at this trial too, where she had repeated the lies, it is inconceivable that they would have brought in the verdict they did.'

Polite disquiet in the legal profession began to be picked up by critical journalists like Bernard Levin, and something had to be done by the judicial establishment to make it seem that the 'unfortunate' 'Lucky' *Gordon* case would not happen again. The Lord Chancellor, with the support of the Lord Chief Justice, quickly introduced a Bill in the House of Lords in January 1964 to allow the Court of Criminal Appeal to order a fresh trial in cases where it upheld an appeal on grounds, for example, that a jury might have reached a different verdict had fresh evidence been before it. This was a sensible enough measure, advocated by Chief Justices for years in statements from the bench, which successive governments had ignored. But it had nothing to do with the real vice of the Court of Appeal's behaviour in *Gordon*, which had been to hide evidence favourable to Ward. But once Keeler had been put away for perjury (in December 1963), Lord Dilhorne introduced the Criminal Appeal Bill in response to what he described as 'the Lord Chief Justice drawing attention to the lack of the power to order a new trial in the recent case of "Lucky" Gordon – a lack which he described in many ways unfortunate.' At a time when he knew that many members of the criminal bar thought that Parker and his court had behaved 'reprehensibly' in the *Gordon* case, Dilhorne went on – 'it is, if I may say so, with the greatest respect to my noble friend the Chief Justice, a great credit to him and his fellow judges that the Court of Criminal Appeal's prestige stands so high'. The Lord Chancellor was followed by the Lord Chief Justice himself. Referring obliquely to criticism of his behaviour he said:

I think that the appeal, perhaps an unfortunate appeal in the case of Aloysius Gordon, did focus attention on the limited powers of the Court of Criminal Appeal. There was, I venture to think, widespread misunderstanding as to the conduct of the trial, but at least I think good has come out of it in that public attention has been focused on the limitation of those powers...

There was no 'widespread misunderstanding' of the 'Lucky' Gordon trial – Keeler's lies on oath had secured the guilty verdict – but there was widespread concern about the Ward trial, to which he may have been obliquely referring. 'Unfortunate' was hardly a sufficient adjective to describe a process that had hidden evidence which would have secured a man's acquittal. Now the government was purporting to cure the defect, to ensure that the 'misfortune' did not happen again by giving the Court of Criminal Appeal the power to order a new trial. But how would this have avoided the 'misfortune' of hiding relevant evidence? On the contrary, as Dilhorne and Parker must have known, it would have hidden it even more deeply and securely – but less controversially.

Had the court ordered, on that morning of Tuesday 30 July, a new trial for Gordon, certain legal

consequences would immediately have followed. He
would not have been freed – he might have applied for
bail, but would probably have been held in prison on
remand. More importantly, the *sub judice* rule would
apply – there would be no mention of the case in the
media until the retrial began, after the summer recess
(i.e. in September or October). Keeler would have
been called, of course, and if she maintained her lies
she would have been discredited and later prosecuted
for perjury as before. But Ward would still have been
convicted on the word of the perjurer, and be several
months into a lengthy prison term. The maximum
sentence for a pimp had recently been increased from
two to five years, and Justice Marshall was well known
for holding quite extreme beliefs about the sinfulness
of prostitution and promiscuity and about the sanctity
of marriage.[38] He could well have sentenced Ward to
five years in prison – three on Count 1 and two on
Count 2, served consecutively. Bestowing a power to

---

38   Judge Gerald Sparrow recalls 'Archie' Marshall, a member of a
     Cambridge Union debating team, with himself and Rab Butler,
     railing about a prostitute they encountered doing business in
     an American hotel. Marshall wore a large gold wedding ring
     (unusual, at the time) which observers at the Ward trial noted
     gave off a golden flash when caught by sunbeams through
     the court windows. See 'The Profumo Affair – Stephen Ward
     speaks, Judge Gerald Sparrow sums up', *Today Magazine*,
     1963, p. 141.

order a new trial on the Court of Criminal Appeal was no answer to the injustice done to Stephen Ward by the behaviour of the Court of Criminal Appeal judges in hiding the evidence – it would simply have ensured that the evidence was hidden more effectively, by the law (the *sub judice* rule) and not by lawyers. The real safeguard against injustice would have to wait another twenty years, and many more miscarriages, until stringent disclosure duties were placed on all prosecutors. The *Ward* case and the Gordon appeal demonstrate that they must, regrettably, be placed on judges as well.

The Summing-up

Mervyn Griffith-Jones ended his closing speech on Tuesday morning with a portentous appeal to the jury to convict Ward as a matter of public interest:

> You may think that the defendant is a thoroughly immoral man for no other reason than he was getting girls for himself and his friends. If you think that this is proved, members of the jury, you may think it is in the highest public interest to do your duty and return a verdict of guilty on this indictment.

Ward was not charged with immorality or with getting girls for himself or his friends, but the moral safety of the people was, for Griffith-Jones, the highest law. The speech was followed by the judge's summing-up. This is the most crucial time for assessing the fairness of any criminal trial in this country. It is always carefully recorded, and it forms the focus of appellate scrutiny. It is essential that it is available to the public because this is the core of the principle of open justice. Lord Parker personally prevented a number of distinguished journalists – Ludovic Kennedy, Lord Kennet and others – from obtaining a copy, although it is known that it was transcribed (along with the evidence) and a copy was sent to Lord Denning, who was at this point preparing his report for the government on the security implications of the Profumo affair. The government still refuses all access to the Denning papers (see Appendix D), although it is now over half a century since his report was released. The CCRC, under Section 17 of the 1995 Act, has power to obtain documents, and should certainly obtain a transcript of the Ward summing-up, which Lord Parker had no right (and arguably no power) to withhold from the public. There is another copy in the National Archives, in a file to which the public, without reason, is denied access.

Ward himself committed suicide on the Tuesday night because he regarded the judge as unbearably biased against him, and most of the commentators who heard the summing-up that day thought it unfair. But they were not lawyers and it would be wrong to assume that an experienced trial judge did not tick the legal boxes thought necessary in 1963 – and more so today – to ensure that a jury is properly directed as to the law and as to how they must approach their task of applying it to the facts. I have scoured all the unofficial reports of the summing-up by Ludovic Kennedy and other journalists and by the Press Association, and they do not mention the judge giving the jury certain directions that were required by law. Some of them, certainly, would be likely to have been reported if they had been given. For example:

• The judge gave no corroboration warning. This was essential, even in 1963: where accomplices are concerned (and Keeler and Rice-Davies, if prostitutes, were Ward's 'accomplices' in law) it was the duty of the judge to warn the jury that it was dangerous to convict on their evidence unless it was corroborated (i.e. confirmed by independent testimony). The judge did mention that these witnesses' evidence required corroboration, but he is not reported as having given the essential warning, or indeed as having told the jury what 'corroboration' was or which testimony by others might amount to it. This was a rule of law in 1963, requiring that a conviction be quashed when the judge did not give the necessary warning and directions.

• There was no clear direction as to what was meant by 'living *in part* on the earnings of prostitution'. The judge eschewed any explanation, and told them it could be a fraction: 'The law laid down no specific percentage.' The law left it to their good sense to say 'whether it had been proved that money which, in part in this case, came from the earnings of prostitution'. This was a misdirection – it meant that the jury could convict if they thought Keeler or Rice-Davies had given a few pounds (or even a few pence) from their 'earnings' to Ward to pay the telephone bill. For reasons explained later, he should have told the jury that 'living on' part of a prostitute's earnings requires them to be sure that the part was sufficient to live on – or at least, amounted to a *significant*, as distinct from minimal, proportion of those earnings.

• Where a defendant is a person of 'good character', i.e. has never been convicted in court before, it is important for the judge to direct the jury that they may take this into account in two ways – it makes it less likely that he would commit an offence, and more likely that he was telling the truth. But the trial judge seemed stumped when he came to this direction. He told the jury he had never come across a case 'when a man says he is of good character when charged with a sexual offence, albeit he says at the same time, "I am an immoral man."' Here, the judge's moral prejudices got the better of his legal duty. The fact that Ward admitted he was promiscuous should not have deprived him of the benefit of the direction – he was not charged with the crime of being immoral, he was charged with living off the earnings of prostitution. It is not against the law to be sexually promiscuous, or even adulterous (and no one in the trial even suggested that Ward's 'utter immorality' stretched to adultery).

• This was a trial that took place amidst such prejudice, with MPs and newspapers continually labelling the women as 'harlots' and 'prostitutes', that the jury had to be warned very carefully about the need to scrutinise the evidence in the case and put out of their minds statements by others, however high their office, who had not heard that evidence and could not determine whether Christine and Mandy were 'women who offered their bodies *indiscriminately* for payment in return for sexual intercourse'. They claimed, of course, to have been discriminating, in the sense that they only had sex with people they liked (and most of the people Keeler liked were unable to pay). But the judge was not reported as giving any clear direction about this, and his warning about the press was no more than a lament about its moral standards, not its capacity to prejudice a trial. As he put it:

> One would have thought, with what we have all been faced with in the national newspapers, that this country has become a sort of sink of iniquity. But you and I know that the even tenor of family life over the overwhelming majority of our population goes quietly and decently on.[39]

The impression given was that those like Ward who gave the press reason to report moral iniquity, should be condemned for disrupting the even tenor of family life by those who represented it. That was what the judge obviously thought. He made no attempt to warn the jury, in terms that are so familiar nowadays and were quite vehement at the outset of the trial of Rebekah Brooks and Andy Coulson in 2013, that they must not be influenced by anything read or heard in the media.

These criticisms of the summing-up, which would all provide grounds for appeal, are made with the caveat that the necessary directions may have been given but were not reported. This can only be decided, one

---

39　Crawford, *The Profumo Affair*, p. 164.

way or the other, by study of the official transcript, irrationally and irresponsibly closed to the public for the foreseeable future. There are two aspects of the summation that are, however, fully reported, and they are fatal to upholding Ward's conviction.

The first relates to Keeler's perjury. The judge, over lunch on the Tuesday, had ample opportunity to think about the Court of Criminal Appeal's decision that morning, and the problem it posed for the fairness of the Ward trial. By this time, Scotland Yard had announced that it was sending the evidence to the DPP, Sir Theo Mathew, to consider prosecuting Keeler for perjury, and it must have been blindingly obvious to Mr Justice Marshall that it would be unfair to convict Ward before there had been an opportunity to test that evidence. But here, from a Press Association report, is what he told the jury:

The appeal has been allowed. The offence with which Gordon was charged was an offence of violence of some kind against Miss Christine Keeler and he had asked that certain witnesses should be present at his trial. These witnesses were sought – you will remember the police answering questions about it and saying they went to many places and were unable to trace them – and they were not called at his trial, but have since been traced and made a statement.

The Appeal Court, he said, had allowed the appeal because they considered it would have been impossible to say that a jury would still have convicted Gordon if these two witnesses had given evidence at his trial. The judge read excerpts from the Lord Chief Justice's remarks to the nodding barristers, and directed the jury: 'The decision of that court you must take to mean involves no assessment of the evidence of Miss Christine Keeler and it has come to no decision on it. It is an extraneous matter and you must exclude it from your minds.'[40]

So the jury were told, authoritatively and as a direction of law, that they must forget all about the Gordon appeal. This made the defence look foolish because Burge had told the jury to take particular note of Keeler's lack of credibility if Gordon's appeal were to succeed. The jury were left blindfolded, unaware that the prosecution witness on whose evidence they were asked to convict Ward, was a perjurer who would, three months later, plead guilty and be sentenced to nine months in prison.

40   Ibid., p. 167.

The other misdirection, which was to prove fatal to Ward and should now prove fatal to his conviction, came on that same Tuesday afternoon. It came just after the judge had dealt with the elements of the offence of living on immoral earnings, contrary to Section 30 of the 1958 Sexual Offences Act, by reading from a very recent judgment of the House of Lords. His legal dissertation would have been quite boring for laypersons, and it must have come as a relief to the jury when these 'directions on law' came to an end. They must have been very attentive when he suddenly announced, 'There is one very important matter to which I want to call your attention. What you make of it is a matter for you.' (This is judicial code for a direction to make something – indeed, much – of it.) The matter was this:

We have not heard, other than Ward himself, one single witness directed to counts one and two, other than possibly the last witness, Jones. The persons involved here, on his story, were his friends. It is a factor the importance of which you must assess for yourselves when you consider the case. There may be many reasons why he has been abandoned in his extremity. You must not guess at them but this is clear: if Stephen Ward was telling the truth in the witness box there are in this city many witnesses

of high estate and low who could have come and
testified in support of his evidence.[41]

This was, no more and no less, a direction to the jury
to speculate, and to infer from the non-appearance
as defence witnesses of many highly (and lowly)
placed persons, that Ward was lying. It was a wrong
– perniciously wrong – direction of a kind that judges
must never give: to find a defendant guilty because of
witnesses they have not seen (but had, perhaps, read
about in the press). Instead of retracting it, he actually spelled out this improper message a little later:
'Many witnesses who could have been called have not
been called in connexion with the defence. They could
have enormously strengthened the case concerning
the earnings of prostitution' (the charges, of course,
on which Ward was convicted).

No appeal court could approve this direction: the
judge was plainly inviting the jury to find that Ward
was lying because he had not called the many witnesses
available in the city to testify in his defence. The
direction was wrong in law, in justice and in reality.
In law, because it invited the jury to use speculation,
not evidence, in order to convict. In justice, because

41   Ibid., p. 169.

Profumo and 'Charles' had not been brought to court by the prosecution and the 'Indian doctor' had issued a public denial but had not been summonsed. Who else did the judge mean – other than Lord Astor, who was not said to have paid when he once had sex with Mandy in Wimpole Mews. And it was wrong in reality, a reality which anyone (other than a judge) would realise and which investigative journalists later discovered. They found that Ward's friends, patients and acquaintances – people like Sir Colin Coote, the Earl of Dudley, Sir Godfrey Nicolson, Sir Gilbert Laithwaite and others of 'high estate' – had met at the Athenaeum Club with Ward's solicitor who asked whether they would at least be prepared to give character evidence for him. They were told that Lord Astor, his closest friend, had been afraid to help, and (as one who was there, a senior foreign office official, told Phillip Knightley):

> If we were seen to be involved in such a sordid case in no matter what role, then we would be destroyed … I can't tell you of the moral awfulness of abandoning a friend when he most needs you, and a friend, moreover, who was completely innocent of the charges against him.[42]

---

42   Knightley and Kennedy, *An Affair of State*, p. 174.

The factual basis of the judge's comment was of course true, as Ward knew and keenly felt – his friends had deserted him, and many left England at this time in case they were subpoenaed. But there were some 'friends' who were in town, and had a public duty to help him, if only because they were public servants. They were the men from MI5, those who had approached him and received information from him and 'watched' his home when it had been visited by Ivanov. Ward's solicitor made frantic attempts to contact 'Woods of the War Office' in room 393 and elsewhere, but there was no response. His evidence would have helped Ward. He visited Wimpole Mews on several occasions during the indictment period, and his recollection of Ward's helpfulness and patriotism would have presented a side that the jury were never allowed to see. Ward claimed in court that he had told MI5 about Keeler and Profumo – and evidence that he did so would have made nonsense of the prosecution claims that he was a pimp, living off her earnings. But MI5 kept very quiet. Its officers had a duty at least to discuss with his solicitor what evidence they might give. So too did the Foreign Office: in 2009 it was revealed that, with the Foreign Secretary's approval, Ward was deployed for national security purposes to feed information through Ivanov to the Soviets. They decided, as his friends and patients had decided at the Athenaeum, not to do the decent thing.

Suicide

That afternoon, Ward was allowed to leave court as usual at 4.30 p.m. (Normally in this period defendants lost their bail once the judge had begun summing-up, and this oversight appears to have been a result of the court clerk's absence.) Ward, unexpectedly free but unexpectedly depressed by what he had already heard of the summing-up, took a taxi to Noel Howard-Jones's flat with his literary agent and the agent's 15-year-old son, whom he asked to run into Boots and obtain a prescription. The young Stephen Pound – now MP for North Ealing – complied, unaware that it was for the ninety-four barbiturate pills ('Nembutal') Ward took that evening, after he had written letters to the judge and prosecutor (never published) and to certain witnesses. His last note, after he had swallowed the pills, was to the law student at whose house he was staying and who was so affected by the trial that he never practised law:

Dear Noel,

I am sorry I had to do this here! It is really more than I can stand – the horror, day after day at the court and in the streets.

It is not only fear, it is a wish not to let them

get me. I would rather get myself. I do hope I have not let people down too much. I tried to do my stuff but after Marshall's summing-up, I've given up all hope. The car needs oil in the gear-box, by the way. Be happy in it.

Incidentally, it was surprisingly easy and required no guts.

I am sorry to disappoint the vultures. I only hope this has done the job. Delay resuscitation as long as possible.[43]

. . .

The next morning, the news of Ward's suicide attempt – he would remain unconscious for the next three days before expiring – was known by the court, and by the jury. Griffith-Jones said there were few precedents (which was true) and suggested that the trial should stand adjourned until the following Tuesday to see whether Ward was well enough to attend. Burge agreed – without Ward in court, he could not take instructions. 'The time for taking instructions is now past,' pronounced the judge. He directed that Ward's bail be withdrawn and that the defendant, in hospital, should be put under police surveillance. He finished his summing-up and sent the jury out to consider their verdict. The hours passed,

43   Crawford, *The Profumo Affair*, p. 170.

placing undue pressure on those jurors who expected to go home at the usual hour, but found themselves obliged to remain until they reached a verdict. At 7.09 p.m., after four and a half hours, they returned to court and convicted the absent Ward on Count 1, and on Count 2.

It was a final act of unfairness, to try a dying man. The time for instructions was not over at all – a defendant has a right to ask the judge, at the end of his summation, to correct factual errors in it, and to consult with his counsel in relation to any jury question (and this jury did ask one very long question, which suggested they had not understood the judge's directions on the 'immoral earnings' charges). The jury were not sent out until after lunch, and would have read the *Evening News* with its account of Ward's suicide attempt. Ludovic Kennedy, who was there, describes the atmosphere that afternoon:

There was a sense of anti-climax, the knowledge that Ward now had no interest in the result of the contest, not even an interest in life itself. There was talk then of his recovery, but the general consensus was that by contracting out as he had done, Ward has immeasurably lessened his chances with the jury ... Perhaps the jury could relax a little, as people do when the man one is talking about goes out of the room, feeling the responsibility lift from them a little, knowing that when the time came for him to hear their verdict, they would not have to endure his searching eyes. They could even ease their consciences a little – and who knows, perhaps they did? – by telling themselves that the attempt at self-destruction was in itself evidence of a guilty mind. Whether the fault was Ward's or not, his absence put him at a disadvantage. It would have been fairer, I think, to have postponed the trial until such time as he could return.[44]

The United Kingdom does not try people *in absentia*. When they run away towards the end of a trial – flee the country, or whatever – the judge has a discretion to allow the trial to continue.[45] It is a discretion that must be exercised judicially, i.e. fairly and reasonably in all the circumstances. Both considerations pointed in Ward's case to an adjournment, but the rush to justice was consistent with the way in which the judge had forced the trial on only nineteen days after the committal, at a time when the prejudice was such that it was impossible for it to be fair.

---

44   Ludovic Kennedy, *The Trial of Stephen Ward* (Penguin, 1963), p. 216.
45   See *R* v. *Jones* [2003] 1 AC 1.

5

GROUNDS OF APPEAL

It will be apparent, from the preceding analysis of the Old Bailey proceedings, that Stephen Ward did not receive 'the birthright of every British citizen', namely a trial that was fair. Although the official transcript of the trial and summing-up has been unaccountably withheld – itself an example of unfairness – the contemporaneous press reports and notes of journalists and authors who attended provide sufficient material at this juncture for the CCRC to commence an investigation, and their statutory powers should be sufficient to obtain the necessary records. With the assistance of Richard Thomas, an experienced criminal barrister, I have drafted the following grounds of appeal, having considered the common and statute law as it applied in 1963 and the requirements for a fair trial, then and now.

As the Court of Appeal has made clear, in considering whether to quash a long-standing conviction, it is the current standard of fairness by which the trial procedure must be judged, however much the conduct of the judge and the lawyers might be excused because they acted in a manner that was condoned in 1963. For example, no complaint can be made about the massively prejudicial publicity from the committal proceedings, because committals at the time were always open to the press, and Ward's case was later used as an example of the need to reform the law so that they could no longer be reported until the trial itself had ended. However, complaint can certainly be made that the prejudicial publicity was such that the trial should not have taken place just nineteen days afterwards – the defence application for a postponement of the trial should have been granted – and an emphatic warning of the danger of being influenced by media sensation should have been given to the jury. In this respect, the publicity is relevant to the question of whether the judge used his discretionary powers in the interests of justice.

Grounds of appeal which would have a 'real possibility of success' can be formulated as follows:

STEPHEN WARD'S CONVICTION WAS UNSAFE,
because:

1. Non-Disclosure of Keeler's Perjury

There was a failure to secure a fair trial by the actions of the prosecution and the Court of Appeal, which had the result of withholding from the jury evidence showing that Christine Keeler was a perjurer.

In one sense, this is what Americans call a 'slam dunk'. Keeler was later prosecuted for her perjury in the Gordon trial, which she had repeated in the Ward trial, and was jailed for nine months. Had Ward lived to lodge an appeal it would have had to be upheld, at least on Count 1. Griffith-Jones assured the jury that in these hypothetical circumstances, the Court of Appeal would put everything right, and the judge did not demur. Even without prosecution misconduct, or non-disclosure, it generally follows that a conviction is quashed when the witness on whose testimony it depends turns out to have committed perjury. In Ward's case, of course, there was serious non-disclosure, even by the standards of the time, abetted by the Court of Appeal itself.

Today, as a result of many trials which have miscarried because of prosecution non-disclosure, there is a strict duty on police (who are part of what is termed 'the apparatus of prosecution') and prosecutors to make all evidence that might be relevant available to the defence. There can be no doubt that evidence of Keeler's perjury was available – Sergeant Burrows, in court and giving evidence in the *Ward* case, presumably would have had in his possession the statements in the *Gordon* case from Fenton and Comacchio and John Hamilton-Marshall, and had taken possession of the incriminating tape. Even in 1963, the rule laid down in the criminal law bible *Archbold* (35th edition, 1962) was that 'where the prosecution have taken a statement from a person whom they know can give material evidence but decide not to call him as a witness, they are under a duty to make that person available to the defence...' It is modern standards of fairness, however, that govern CCRC applications, requiring all material statements to be handed over to the defence. Today there would be no mystery – the Gordon appeal would be heard before the Ward trial, and the fact that Keeler was a perjurer would make the prosecutor pause about putting her forward as a witness of truth. The behaviour of the Lord Chief Justice and his colleagues in upholding Gordon's appeal without giving reasons (which would have revealed the evidence), and declaring in effect that their decision cast no shadow on her credibility, remains the most serious allegation of misconduct made in modern times against Britain's senior judiciary.

The judges must have known, from the saturation coverage of the *Ward* trial, exactly what stage it had reached, and their decision not to test or reveal the evidence, and to misrepresent its force, cries out for condemnation. It may be that the Court of Appeal members were acting out of misplaced caution, having determined to do or say nothing that would affect the *Ward* trial in favour of either prosecution or defence, believing that their role was to allow it to take its unimpeded course and to cure any defect on appeal. This was a bad mistake – it should have been obvious to these judges that the evidence in their possession would assist the defence, and they had a duty to ensure that the defence had an opportunity to make use of it. By pretending that the appeal result cast no doubt on Keeler's veracity, however, they unfairly undermined Ward's defence.

There could be an explanation for the behaviour of the prosecuting counsel. These were minor criminal charges, usually tried at Quarter Sessions, and as such did not directly involve the Director of Public Prosecutions (then, the notably fair Sir Theo Mathew). The case was brought by police, and counsel would have been 'briefed' only by a police solicitor, Mr Griffith-Jones, an aloof man, famed for his reluctance to speak even to his own witnesses (including police officers), may not have been told by Herbert of the evidence that had mounted against Keeler in the *Gordon* case. Or, it may be that he was simply blinded by his own contempt for Ward's 'utter immorality' – he prosecuted with a fervour unbefitting counsel who are meant to be 'ministers of justice'. There may be other explanations, including failures by the defence. There is no doubt that Mr Burge was aware of the point because he invited Keeler to repeat her perjured evidence, and in his final speech he invited the jury to take note of the result of the next day's *Gordon* appeal, so he must have had a shrewd idea that the verdict would be overturned. But after the Court of Criminal Appeal decision he does not appear to have applied for an adjournment so the evidence would be re-opened. One of the bad practices at the Old Bailey in those days was for counsel to see the judge in private (although with a shorthand writer present) and there may have been behind-the-scenes dealings. If so, they should now be exposed.

One advantage of a CCRC reference is that the commission will be able to obtain through its discovery powers the material in the briefs for counsel on both sides; transcripts of any secret 'in chambers' meetings with the judge; witness statements and the tape transcript that were hidden in the Gordon appeal; any correspondence by or to the Lord Chief Justice about transmitting his remarks in that appeal to Mr Justice Marshall. This might clear up questions about why the Court of Criminal Appeal and the judge and counsel in the trial acted as they did – it would not, of course, detract from the fact that, as a result of their actions, a grave injustice was done to Stephen Ward. One would like to think that, had he lived, this injustice would have been rectified on appeal, at least by the quashing of Count 1 which depended on Keeler's evidence. By that time, of course, Ward would have served some months in prison.

2. Fresh Evidence

Post-trial evidence, namely Keeler's conviction, proves her perjury.

This is a different, and less controversial, way of putting the non-disclosure point. The evidence of Keeler's perjury conviction could not, obviously, have been called at Ward's trial, since she was not prosecuted until after it ended. The evidence on which the prosecution was based did not go before Ward's jury – this was prevented by the action of the Chief Justice.

In any appeal, a defendant can call new evidence if it satisfies the four admissibility criteria in Section 23 (2) of the Criminal Appeal Act 1968:

- it is capable of belief – obviously: it is a conviction, with the documents to support it;
- it gives rise to a ground of appeal – plainly, as Keeler was the principal witness on Count 1;
- it would have been admissible at the trial – certainly, to prove Keeler a liar;
- there is a good explanation for why it was not used at the trial – because the evidence had not been disclosed and the conviction came after the trial.

As Mr Griffith-Jones told the jury, if there was any issue about Keeler's credibility in respect of the *Gordon* case, it could be put right on appeal. After half a century, it is time that it was.

3. Speculation about Absent Friends

The judge erroneously directed the jury that they could infer Ward's guilt from the friends, 'high and low', whom he declined to call.

This was a palpable misdirection, given at an important stage of the summing-up, and repeated so the jury would pay maximum attention to it. Juries must never be told to speculate, or to infer a man's guilt from the absence of friends he might have called, or to disbelieve his evidence because he did not call hypothetical witnesses to back it up. The judge specifically related this direction to Ward's guilt on the 'immoral earnings' counts on which he was in due course convicted, and experienced court commentators like Ludovic Kennedy described it as devastatingly prejudicial. It was not even logical, in its terms, because friends and acquaintances would not have been there on the occasion when Keeler alleged that Ward had encouraged her to have sex with 'Charles', and would not know whether the few pounds she contributed to the telephone bill had come from the banknotes she had been handed by Profumo as 'a little something for your mother'. They could not tell, even if they observed Mandy handing over her £6 rent, whether it came from her £80 a week stipend from Rachman or from the grateful Indian doctor. Besides which, a decision not to give evidence for a friend may be made from fear of public embarrassment and not from knowledge that the friend was lying. This appears to be precisely the reason why his patients and clients decided, at the Athenaeum meeting, not to expose themselves to public shame.

The appeal on this ground requires no work by the CCRC, although of course it would benefit from having the official transcript of the summing-up. This misdirection, which many believe tipped Ward to suicide, is reported verbatim in most books about the trial.

4. No Corroboration Warning

The judge erred in failing to give a proper corroboration direction.

Even in 1963 – indeed, for a century before that – the criminal law, so harsh on criminals, had also developed an aversion to their accomplices when they were called as Crown witnesses, and it had no confidence in the testimony of prostitutes. Since Christine and Mandy were both, on the prosecution's case (they were 'accomplices' because they had given Ward their immoral earnings to live on) the judge had a solemn legal duty to warn the jury about accepting their evidence. He had to tell them in terms that it was *doubly dangerous* to convict on the evidence of an accomplice prostitute unless it was 'corroborated'. He had to define 'corroboration' so lay people could understand it (many lawyers and judges, as the cases show, do not). In 1963, the law required him to instruct the jury that:

what is required is some independent testimony
which affects the prisoner by tending to connect
him with the crime; that is, evidence, direct or
circumstantial, which implicates the prisoner, which
confirms in some material particular not only the
evidence given by the accomplice that the crime
has been committed but also that the prisoner
committed it.[46]

Moreover, the judge had to point out to the jury the
evidence given in the trial that was capable in law of
being regarded as corroboration.[47] In particular, in
this case he was obliged to tell them very clearly that
Keeler's evidence on Count 1 could not corroborate
Rice-Davies's evidence on Count 2, or vice versa.[48]

Although these requirements for the summing-up
originated from a rule of practice, by 1963 it had hard-
ened into a rule of law. If the warning was not given, the
conviction had to be quashed, no matter how ample the
corroboration was in fact.[49] It is strongly arguable that
there was no corroboration of either woman's evidence
that they gave Ward any of the money that came from

---

46   R v. *Baskerville* [1916] 2 KB 658.
47   R v. *Clynes* [1960] 44 Cr App R 158.
48   R v. *Noakes* [1832] 5 C & P 326.
49   *Davies* v. *DPP* [1954] AC 378.

'Charles', or from Eynan or Profumo, or from 'the Indian doctor', so this point could be made an additional and separate ground of appeal. But on the law as it stood in 1963 (and stands now) the failure of the judge to give the prostitute/accomplice corroboration warning would be fatal to the conviction. While Mr Justice Marshall told the jury they must find corroboration, he does not seem to have told them what it was, where they might find it, or why it was dangerous to convict on an accomplice's evidence, or that one accomplice could not corroborate another. This ground of appeal cannot be confidently advanced until the transcript of the summing-up is obtained, so the judge's failure to give the appropriate direction can be verified.

5. No Good Character Direction

The judge failed to direct the jury as to Ward's good character, and instead told them that he was a person of bad character, because he had admitted to being 'immoral'.

Today it is essential to direct the jury that the fact that a defendant has no previous convictions makes it (i) less likely that he would have any propensity to commit the offence charged and (ii) more likely that his evidence would be true.[50] (Some judges add a

---

50   *R* v. *Vye & Ors* [1993] 97 Cr App R 134.

reminder that 'every criminal has to be convicted for a first time'.) It was not essential, in 1963, to give a good character direction in every case: as *Archbold* puts it, 'the fact that the judge makes no reference to the good character of the prisoner does not neces-sarily amount to a misdirection'.[51] It certainly did in *Ward*, however, because the judge told the jury of what he considered a paradox that he had never come across before, namely that Ward's good character was effectively cancelled out by his bad character, because he had confessed to being 'immoral'.

This was plainly wrong. Ward had never been in trouble with the law, a fact which the jury should have been told to take into account on the question of his propensity to break it. His admission of 'immoral-ity' was no more than an admission to promiscuity, which was not a crime (except, it seems, in the eyes of the judge and Mr Griffith-Jones). Mr Justice Marshall misunderstood the purpose of a good character direc-tion, which is to give presumptive credit to a defendant who has kept out of trouble all his life, and by telling the jury in effect that Ward did not deserve it because he had admitted immorality, he was being illogical as

---

51 *Archbold: Criminal Pleading, Evidence and Practice*, 35th edn (Sweet & Maxwell, 1962), 919620 p. 565, citing *R* v. *Aberg* [1948] 2KB 173.

well as prejudicial. He seemed to be telling the jury that Ward was a person of 'bad' character, and hence more likely to commit a sexual offence.

6. What is a 'Part' of a Prostitute's Earnings?

The judge failed to direct the jury that they could only convict if satisfied that Ward was living mainly or in significant part (or at least to some discernible extent) on the earnings of prostitutes.

Section 30 of the Sexual Offences Act made it an offence for a man (although not for a woman) 'knowingly to live wholly or in part on the earnings of prostitution'. This was how pimps were prosecuted, as the textbook of the time, the 35th edition of *Archbold*, explained: 'this is usually proved by evidence that the prostitute paid the rent of rooms where both were living together, or paid for the prisoner's food, or supplied him with money, or paid for drink consumed by him in public houses, or the like'. Such cases were a world away from Ward, who was in no real sense living on Mandy or Christine's earnings, but rather accommodating them and accepting small payments for the phone bill and the return of loans he had made to them. Even if they were prostitutes, it should not have been a crime for a friend or cohabitant to accept small amounts of money from them, be it a contribution to the phone bill or a can of beans for the larder. Section 30 must have had some common-sense limitation. The judge expressly declined to give it any limitation – 'in part' meant in *any* part – 'if only a fraction of his income was produced in this way it would be sufficient'.[52] This cannot be right: English law adopts, as a matter of statutory construction, the principle *de minimis non curat lex*, the law does not concern itself with trifles or, for that matter, with fractions.

The judge's interpretation of 'in part' leads to the absurdity that accepting a few coins for the gas meter, or a few pounds in rent, turns a prostitute's cohabitee or landlord into a pimp. 'To live in part on the earnings of prostitution' must mean 'to live to some extent on' or 'to live in significant part' – it cannot mean 'to live in the tiniest fractional part on…' 'Living on' earnings carries the connotation of having enough to live on from these earnings, and 'a part' as contrasted with a whole is certainly not a mere fraction. As a result of this misdirection, the jury would have thought they could convict Ward if Keeler and Rice-Davies gave him a few pence towards the telephone bill. It is absurd to say that a professional man earning £4,000 from his practice and £1,500 from his portraiture (totalling £100,000 in today's money) was living *on* their earnings.

---

52   Clive Irving, Ron Hall and Jeremy Wallington, *Scandal '63* (Heinemann, 1963), p. 201.

This was precisely the kind of conviction that the Wolfenden Committee in its report on sexual offences had sought to avoid, because it would mean that prostitutes could never knowingly be befriended or supplied with basic necessities. It paraphrased 'in whole or in part' as living 'wholly or mainly' on the tainted earnings, which is obviously what Parliament meant when it passed Section 30 in 1956. The judge made a crucial mistake of law, which must have had an impact on the jury because once the prosecution proves that a woman is a prostitute and the defendant has assisted her trade, Section 30 throws the burden of proving that he is *not* living on her earnings on the defence. So under the judge's misdirection, the jury would have thought that Ward had to prove that he did not receive a *fraction* of Christine or Mandy's hand-outs from the men with whom they had sex. This would explain their otherwise inexplicable 'guilty' verdicts, and is a particularly compelling reason why they should be overturned.

7. Insufficient Evidence

The convictions on Counts 1 and 2 cannot be sustained by the evidence.

Quite apart from the misdirection about receiving a 'fraction' of their earnings, there is a further substantive appeal point – namely that Ward was in fact innocent. The evidence from all the reports of the trial (and Ludovic Kennedy gives a reasonably full account of every witness) was insufficient to establish a link between the women's payments to Ward and the origin of the money in their earnings from prostitution. Keeler, it is true, had no obvious means of support (other than occasional fees from modelling) except for the £50 from Charles, the £20 from Profumo and the £100 or so pounds in total received from Mr Eynan. But she lived rent-free, received loans from Ward, and specifically said that she paid him occasionally only to reduce her debt to him. Repayment by a prostitute of a loan from a man cannot implicate that man in living on her earnings, at least unless he is proved to know that the money came from her sex work.

As for Mandy, she spent only six weeks at the flat, paying four weeks' rent (£24) in advance, evidently from the lavish allowance she had been, and still was, receiving from Rachman. If this was the earnings of prostitution, it was not earned at Wimpole Mews, which was the allegation the prosecution had to prove. It is unclear from the evidence whether her earnings from 'the Indian doctor' in return for sex were given to Ward, and if she did give money to him whether it came from Savundra or from the Rachman stipend which continued until the latter's death in late November.

The conviction on each count was unsafe, in other words, because there was insufficient evidence to support it. The judge in these circumstances should have withdrawn Counts 1 and 2 from the jury (and Counts 4 and 5 should never have been put before them) either at the close of the prosecution's case or at the end of the evidence. There is no report that James Burge made any application for this, but that is not necessary – as the case of John Stonehouse (the MP who walked into the water in Miami and washed up with his mistress in Melbourne) confirmed, a trial judge has a duty to stop an insufficient prosecution of his own motion. It would have been a courageous step to take, given that the government, the opposition and the media were all in full cry against Ward, but an independent and fair judge would have done it. 'Archie' Marshall was not in that category: his Christian commitment to 'the even tenor of family life' as the highest good made him antipathetic to Stephen Ward whose promiscuity so challenged it. Marshall believed Ward to be guilty and believed that his guilt should be established as quickly as possible.

8. They Were Not 'Prostitutes' Anyway

Neither Christine Keeler nor Marilyn Rice-Davies were 'prostitutes' within the meaning of the law during the time charged in the indictment.

When Parliament passed the 1958 Sexual Offences Act, it unaccountably failed to provide a statutory definition of 'prostitute'. Keeler and Rice-Davies emphatically denied that they were prostitutes, and the judge invited Ward to give his definition, which turned (reasonably enough) on whether the woman was having sex with any affection or pleasure or merely as a business arrangement. The jury were, so it seems from reports of the summing-up, left to decide whether Mandy and Christine were 'selling their bodies indiscriminately for profit'. On the evidence they were certainly discriminating in their lovers: Keeler pointed out that she could have made a fortune by selling herself to high bidders. Instead, over the Count 1 period, she had sex with four impoverished boyfriends – the law student Noel Howard-Jones, a Persian youth, 'Lucky' Gordon and then Johnny Edgecombe, plus those who paid her: Profumo (who gave her unrequested gifts of a cigarette lighter and £20), 'Charles' (whom she said she liked and with whom she had sex only once, and not at Wimpole Mews) and Mr Eynan, who knew her previously and who took her out on the town as an attractive escort and had sex with her at the mews 'three or four times over the period of a year'. This was not an 'indiscriminate' or 'arbitrary' clientele: if a prostitute is a member of the oldest profession, Keeler was certainly not a professional. Many thought of her as a 'good-time girl', who would only have sex with someone attractive, or, in the case of Profumo and 'Charles' Clore, with someone important. She certainly did not make herself routinely or arbitrarily available for sex to those who would pay for it.

As for Mandy Rice-Davies, the label was even less appropriate. She had been 'kept' by Rachman as a mistress, with a flat and car and stipend of £80 a week which continued over into the first few weeks of her Wimpole Mews occupancy. After his death in November she said she moved on to 'the Indian doctor', who was looking for an available woman to serve as a mistress. But she did not go to bed with him until she had met him and decided she liked him, and she ended the relationship after two weeks when she decided she did not like him enough to continue. He paid her £25 at first, a sum which was offered as a payment for her acting lessons. She was discerning with her lovers, and did not have sex with Savundra for a fee that was fixed beforehand. She was not 'selling her body indiscriminately for sex'.

Profumo, Eynan and 'Charles' were not under any obligation to pay Keeler, and Savundra paid Mandy with the intention or at least hope of acquiring her exclusive sexual services, by perhaps paying her rent for the flat so he could visit her there a few times a week when Ward was out. Neither woman could accurately be described as a 'prostitute', then or now. Mandy may not have been 'discriminating' in any qualitative sense – Rachman as a Notting Hill landlord gave his name to vicious stand-over tactics to extirpate inconvenient tenants, and Savundra turned out to be a swindler – but she was eighteen and wanted to marry Rachman and was initially attracted to Savundra, not for money (she was still receiving her stipend from Rachman) but because she enjoyed having sex.

In other words, the jury got it wrong – confused, perhaps, by the word 'indiscriminate' and thinking that it might be satisfied merely by evidence that the women were promiscuous, rather than in the business of selling sex indiscriminately or arbitrarily to all or most comers. These young women made choices that were always very calculated, and were never arbitrary.

9. No Guilty Mind

There was no evidence that Ward knew that the women were prostitutes or that he knew they were

paying him for services that he would not have
supplied but for the fact that they were prostitutes.

The whole purpose of making it a crime for a man
to live on a prostitute's earnings is to punish pimps,
or 'ponces' as they were known in 1963 (before the
meaning of that word changed to mean fashionable upstarts given to flashy or effeminate 'poncing
around') for being parasites on sex workers. The
judges had recently applied it to the publisher of
The Ladies' Directory,[53] a 'Who's Who' of London
prostitutes who paid for its advertisements from
their earnings. They ruled that in Section 30 cases the
prosecution had to prove that the defendant 'knowingly assisted' the sex work – that he supplied goods
or services for the purpose of prostitution 'which they
would not be supplied with *but for* the fact that they
were prostitutes'. The judge in his summing-up, and
again in answer to a question posed by the jury after
several hours' retirement, gave them a perfectly correct
definition on this point of 'knowing assistance'. But
how could any jury have decided, on the evidence,
that Ward provided the women with services (e.g.
the spare bedroom) knowing they were prostitutes or
because they were prostitutes?

---

53   *Shaw* v. *DPP* [1963] AC 220.

Ward himself never had sex with Keeler. He said he did not know Profumo had paid her and would have been shocked had he known – it was Profumo's power, not his money, that was the attraction. (In any event, the 'little something for your mother' appears to have been a spontaneous present.) He met Eynan only once, as he was leaving for his surgery, and assumed he was an acquaintance, not a paying client. Keeler did not allege that Ward knew she was paid by Eynan. As for 'Charles', she did make that allegation and he denied it, but in any event (i) she was a perjurer; (ii) it happened only once; and (iii) the sex did not take place, as charged, at Wimpole Mews; and (iv) there was no evidence that he knew, when Keeler repaid part of his loan, that the money had come from 'Charles' and had been paid to her for sexual services.

As for Mandy, Ward allowed her to rent his spare room at an undervalue, not at the excessive rent usual for a landlord who knows his tenant is soliciting. Although they had once had sex at Cliveden back in 1961, she had then become Rachman's mistress (which did not count as 'prostitution' or at least was not charged in Count 2). After his death and her suicide attempt, Ward allowed her parents to stay at the mews to nurse her – not because he knew she was a prostitute, but because he was kind.

As for Savundra, Mandy alleged that Ward knew the man was looking to rent a room in order to have a regular assignation with a girlfriend, and invited Mandy to meet him to decide whether she wanted to be that girl. Ward denied this allegation, but even taken at face value it did not mean that he was allowing Mandy to stay *only* because she was a prostitute. She had been Rachman's mistress, had quarrelled with her 'sugar daddy' and decided – although she said she still loved him – to flee his rent-free nest. She was a friend, and Dr Ward helped her out with accommodation. This all happened in October/November 1962 in the weeks before her suicide attempt and there is no evidence that any part of the money she received from Savundra in that period was ever paid to Ward. He said that she paid no rent in those weeks, and anything she gave him for the telephone or for food could have come from her Rachman retainer.

If the case is referred, the Court of Appeal must apply the test for whether a conviction is 'safe' that was laid down by Lord Bingham in relation to CCRC references: 'if the Court, although by no means persuaded of an appellant's innocence, is subject to some lurking doubt or uneasiness whether injustice has been done (or) if, on consideration of all the facts and circumstances of the case before it, the Court entertains real doubts whether the appellant was guilty of the offence of which he has been convicted, the Court will consider the conviction unsafe.'[54]

On other grounds, the doubts jump out and shock. On this ground, they definitely lurk.

10. Continuing in Ward's Absence

The judge erred in continuing the trial after the defendant's suicide attempt.

The judge has a discretion to deal with unexpected circumstances that occur in the course of a trial, but he must exercise that discretion reasonably and with fairness to the defendant. There was no need for haste – the problem presented itself on Wednesday morning, at a time when it was thought that, with the help of stomach-pumping, Ward might be back in court the following Tuesday. Both counsel requested an adjournment, but the judge refused – he wanted a verdict that night, whether Ward recovered or not. By lunchtime Ward's situation was known to be perilous, but the summing-up continued and then the jury was sent out to consider its verdict. On basic principles, the judge was wrong to reject the adjournment

---

54   *Ex parte Pearson* [2000] 1 Cr App R 141 at 146.

requested by both sides. A defendant's attempted suicide cannot be equated with a defendant's deliberate escape. The former is an action taken (as the old verdict of suicide put it) 'when the balance of the mind is disturbed' and the defendant seeks to inflict upon himself the ultimate penalty, while the latter is a deliberate attempt to avoid punishment. If at all possible, trials must proceed in the presence of the defendant – his 'British birthright' (now guaranteed by the European Convention) is not only to have a fair trial but to attend it, and the judge has a duty to effectuate that right if reasonably possible. This refusal to adjourn produced a situation where the jury might well have thought that his suicide attempt amounted to a confession of guilt.

11. Unfair Trial

The judge failed to secure a fair trial for Stephen Ward in the face of massive adverse publicity and the buying up of witnesses, whether by acceding to a request to adjourn the trial or by warning of the dangers of public prejudice.

It can safely be said that there has been no criminal trial in modern British history where a defendant has had so much prejudicial publicity in the weeks before its commencement. From the time of Mr Profumo's personal statement to Parliament in March until his retraction on 5 June there was a spate of media stories about Ward and critical comments by politicians, and this became a barrage once the libel risks lifted with Profumo's confession. The outpourings of scandal from the committal proceedings began on 28 June, preceded by the Profumo debate in the House of Commons on 17 June where Ward was labelled as a Soviet intermediary, a Russian agent and a Soviet spy and the women were called, by MP after MP, 'prostitutes', 'whores' and 'harlots'. Keeler's 'story' was bought, ghosted and published by the *News of the World*, for a sum equivalent today to £400,000, and Mandy sold titbits to other publications and admitted at the trial that she was hoping to make a lot of money. The prejudice that had been whipped up was evidenced by the angry crowds outside both the magistrates' court and the Old Bailey. The judge rejected a defence application to postpone the trial, rushing it on only nineteen days after the committal. He does not appear to have given the jury any specific warning about the danger of convicting on the evidence of witnesses bought up by the media and who were hoping to make large amounts of money for stories that could only be published without libel risk if Ward were convicted. This warning was regarded as essential in more recent cases where the media paid 'blood money' to witnesses – the trials of Jeremy Thorpe and Rosemary West and Rebekah Brooks, for example – and it was essential in Ward's case as well. The judge vaguely lamented how the press was portraying a climate of immorality in Britain, but does not appear to have warned the jury about the dangers in this climate of convicting the defendant merely because he was 'immoral', rather than proved beyond reasonable doubt to have lived parasitically on prostitutes.

Publicity which irredeemably prejudices a defendant in the eyes of the jury requires a conviction to be quashed if it has not been negated or ameliorated by directions in the judge's summing-up. That was the reason why the 'Winchester Three' convictions were overturned, because the loquacious Lord Denning had gone on television to say that IRA defendants who refused to give evidence are all guilty, shortly after the defendants at this IRA-related trial declined to give evidence.[55] It was one reason why the conviction of the Taylor sisters was quashed after their guilt on a murder charge had been insinuated by *The Sun*.[56] The current law, which would be applied on

---

55   R v. *McCann* [1991] 92 Cr App R 239.
56   R v. *Taylor and Taylor* [1994] 98 Cr App R 361.

appellate reconsideration of the fairness of the Ward trial, is that the conviction must be quashed if either:

a) The risk of prejudice was so grave that whatever measures were adopted by the judge, the trial process could not reasonably be expected to remove it,[57] or

b) If the prejudice could have been removed by appropriate action within the trial process, and the judge did not take those actions.[58]

These tests are not easy to satisfy. *R* v. *Ward* is a rare case, like the 'Winchester Three' and the Taylor sisters, where a) is arguably applicable. Certainly b) would stand a reasonable success on appeal, because Marshall did not use the procedures available – an adjournment until after the summer vacation, or powerful warnings to the jury – to ameliorate the prejudice. The conviction of Abu Hamza (the 'case of the hook-handed cleric') was only upheld because appropriate measures had been taken by the judge to negate tabloid demonisation of the defendant. In Ward's case, his demonisation as a Soviet spy and 'procurer of popsies for the upper classes' had come not merely from the *News of the World,* but from lords and MPs in Parliament, from *The Times* and *The Guardian* (although not from *The Observer,* still

---

57   *Montgomery* v. *HM Advocate* [2003] 1 AC 641 (PC).

58   *R* v. *Abu Hamza* [2007] 1 Cr App R 27.

owned by the Astor family) and from assorted bishops and clerics and public pontificators. If it was possible to ameliorate this prejudice, the judge seems to have made no attempt to do so.

12. Abuse of Process

The prosecution of Stephen Ward was unconstitutional, and his trial an abuse of process, because it was instigated by the government through the direction of the Home Secretary.

The concept of 'abuse of process' – broadly, the use of legal proceedings in bad faith or as a result of unlawful actions by officials – was developing in the early 1960s[59] and is now an established ground for stopping a trial in its tracks or derailing a conviction. The evidence that Home Secretary Sir Henry Brooke directed the Metropolitan Police Commissioner to begin an investigation and prosecution of Ward, after being told that MI5 did not have the evidence to proceed against him under the Official Secrets Act, hinges on the minutes of the meeting that took place between them on 27 March 1963. These minutes were referred to in Lord Denning's report, with further detail (based on a 'semi-official leak' from MI5)

59   See *Connolly* v. *DPP* [1964] AC 1254 (HL).

provided by Nigel West in 1972[60] and by Knightley and Kennedy in 1987.[61] The official minutes, however, have not been released, and the extent to which the Home Secretary directed the Commissioner to 'get Ward' is unclear. The CCRC can obtain the full minutes under its discovery powers.

What is wrong – indeed, unconstitutional – about police acting under the instructions of the executive? The principle was set out by Lord Denning, in *Raymond Blackburn's Case* in 1968:

It is the duty of the Commissioner (of Metropolitan Police) to enforce the law of the land … so that honest citizens may go about their affairs in peace. But in all these things, he is not the servant of anyone, save of the law itself. No minister of the Crown can tell him that he must, or must not, prosecute this man or that one. Nor can any police authority tell him so. The responsibility for law enforcement lies on him. He is answerable to the law and to the law alone.[62]

---

60   Nigel West, *A Matter of Trust: MI5 1945–72* (Weidenfeld & Nicolson, 1972), p. 96.

61   Knightley and Kennedy, *An Affair of State*, pp. 163–4.

62   *R* v. *Commissioner of Police of the Metropolis, ex parte Blackburn* [1968] 2 QB 118 at 136.

In later cases, it was accepted that a police chief must have complete operational control of his force, and that neither the police authority nor the Secretary of State may give him directions about who he should or should not investigate or prosecute.[63] The principle was applied by the Privy Council in 2013, when declaring that the Prime Minister of Antigua had acted unlawfully and unconstitutionally in giving directions to his Police Commissioner to stop a trespass on Crown land.[64] It is fundamental in a Westminster democracy that government ministers do not give orders to police to investigate anyone – yet that seems precisely what the Home Secretary did when he urged the Police Commissioner to investigate Ward.

The unconstitutional direction given by the government on 27 March 1963, without which there would never have been an investigation or an ensuing prosecution, would make that trial an abuse of process. The investigation instigated by the Home Secretary involved the tapping of Ward's telephone (which would have had to be personally approved by the Home Secretary himself), the 'watching' of his home and surgery, and the intrusive interviewing of his

---

63   R v. *Secretary of State for the Home Department, ex parte Northumberland Police Authority* [1989] QB 26 at 39.

64   *Antigua Power Co Ltd* v. *Attorney General* [2013] UKPC 23.

patients and clients and friends and women. These were measures that should only be inflicted on those suspected of serious crime. It was an abuse of power to deploy them to drum up evidence so that Stephen Ward could be tried as a pimp.

There may be grounds of appeal to be added (or subtracted) after a short CCRC investigation. I have made no reference to allegations about the oppressive nature of the police investigation – the twenty-four times they interviewed Keeler, the subterfuges said to have been used against Mandy Rice-Davies (including remand to Holloway on a driving licence charge and a bogus threat to prosecute her over a rented television) because these were canvassed by the defence at the trial. Although they were dismissed by the trial judge with the familiar disclaimer ('of course, members of the jury, it's a matter for you...'), they were in evidence and probably influenced the jury to acquit on Count 3. Chief Inspector Herbert's cruel threats to Ronna Ricardo, to take away her baby and put her young sister in a remand home unless she gave false evidence at the preliminary hearing, were exposed when she bravely refused to commit perjury at the Old Bailey. But we may hear more about Herbert. He was promoted for his efforts in the *Ward* case to become a superintendent but died from a heart attack in 1966, whereupon it was discovered that he had a secret stash of £30,000 (half a million pounds, in today's money). It could only have come from corrupt payments, and a Scotland Yard investigation was duly commenced. The CCRC should find out what happened to it, and whether the source of the money might have been a multimillionaire – Charles Clore, for example, or Dr Emil Savundra, grateful to Chief Inspector Herbert for keeping their names out of the case and their bodies out of the witness box. I do not suggest that Mr Burrows was guilty of any impropriety – indeed he seems to have done a commendable job in gathering evidence of Keeler's perjury in the *Gordon* case and he would not have been responsible for the failure of the prosecutor and of the Court of Appeal to disclose it.

This is not a case that requires further or 'fresh' evidence – the fifty-year-old testimony at the Old Bailey is ample to establish the wrongfulness of Ward's conviction. The two crucial prosecution witnesses would still be available, although in my opinion it would be unnecessary to take a fresh statement from Christine Keeler. She has recently lent her name to books claiming that Ward, although not her pimp, was a Soviet spymaster, meeting not only Ivanov but Anthony Blunt and Roger Hollis, who would join him in the mews – not to make up a bridge four, but to plot the downfall of Western civilisation. These allegations about Hollis echo those by Peter 'Spycatcher' Wright and Chapman Pincher, who claimed that the head of MI5 in 1963 was a Soviet spy – a claim that has received no support from KGB and GRU archives, and is now generally disbelieved. Mandy Rice-Davies, on the other hand, has made what she terms 'a slow descent into respectability', and lives with her husband of twenty-seven years in their house at Virginia Waters. She has consistently maintained Ward's innocence, and in her first book on the subject, published in January 1964, she asserted, 'He most certainly never influenced me to sleep with anyone, nor ever asked me to do so.' In that event, of course, Ward's conviction on Count 2 would have to be quashed, because it was based on the allegation that he influenced her to have sex with Savundra, a decision for which, today, she emphatically takes sole responsibility.

6

OVER TO THE CCRC

The Stephen Ward case, like the Profumo affair to which it is umbilically attached, still arouses strong emotions and real concerns, fifty years on. At a brief debate in the House of Lords in 2013, reproduced in Appendix D, demands were made for the release of the Denning papers but were rebuffed by the government spokesman because 'there are still some sensational personal items in here'. Lord Armstrong, formerly Mrs Thatcher's Cabinet Secretary who travelled the world in an attempt to stop the publication of *Spycatcher* (and who was forced to admit in the witness box in Sydney that he had been 'economical with the truth'), demanded that the Denning papers be embargoed for a century – i.e. until 2063. Whatever view one takes of British secrecy obsessions, they must be trumped by British determination to do justice. What must be released – either from the

Denning papers or the National Archives – is the trial transcript, which cannot conceivably be regarded as confidential.

The conduct and fairness of the trial has been authoritatively called into question. Sir David Tudor Price, the High Court judge who had been junior counsel to James Burge, said in 1985 that Lord Parker acted 'reprehensibly' to undermine Ward's defence – an extraordinarily serious allegation to be made by a sitting judge against a former Chief Justice (see Appendix A).[65] Lord Goodman, the eminent solicitor, advised the publishers of Ludovic Kennedy's book and had to investigate its claims: he found the prosecution the most outrageous he had ever encountered (Appendix B).[66] Bernard Levin's attack on the trial, in his book *The Pendulum Years* (Appendix C), remains not only a superb example of polemic, but the statement of a case against the Court of Appeal that only the Court of Appeal can answer.[67] In all the other books published about Ward – even the ghost-ridden and ghost-written memoirs of Mandy and Christine – the authors have concluded that he was not guilty as charged.

---

65   Knightley and Kennedy, *An Affair of State*, p. 239 and p. 252.
66   Arnold Goodman, *Tell them, I'm On My Way* (Chapmans, 1993), p. 174.
67   Levin, *The Pendulum Years* (Pan Books, 1972), pp. 82–5.

Fifty years on, a reference to the Court of Appeal by the CCRC is not only desirable but essential if that body is to live up to the purpose expressed by Lord Chief Justice Bingham in the *Derek Bentley* case. That reference implicated a Chief Justice, Lord Goddard, half a century before, in manipulating the unfair trial of a mentally handicapped youth, and a Home Secretary who sent him to the gallows heedless of the jury's recommendation of mercy. (It is almost unbearable, today, to read of his death cell parting with his mother.) The CCRC's power of reference allowed the Court of Appeal to make amends for this historic injustice. Stephen Ward took his life by his own hand, but the forces that drove him to it had a grip on the legal system that must never be permitted again.

There may be concerns about taking up the time of the Court of Appeal when there are arguably innocent people in prison awaiting their turn. The obvious answer is that this case does not require the kind of exegesis that was necessary in *Bentley* or *Hanratty*: all that is required are the official transcripts of evidence on Counts 1 and 2 (which took less than two days of actual testimony) and the official transcript of the judge's summing-up, which took five hours. Once these are obtained, the main grounds of appeal can be advanced through these documents and argued within

a day. There would be no need to go into the historical background. The Court of Appeal has sounded
a note of concern about 'historical' references – in
Ruth Ellis for example, and in *Hanratty*[68] (a conviction forty years before) it remarked that there had to
be 'exceptional circumstances to justify incurring the
expenditure of resources on this scale'. But it was
speaking of a reference that involved a massive inquiry
into the circumstances of a complex murder prosecution, which had even involved exhuming the body of
the hanged man to enable extensive evidence from
DNA experts. The court's judgment took sixty-two
closely printed pages, after two weeks of argument.
As for the need for 'exceptional circumstances', there
is no case in the modern history of English criminal
trials as exceptional as that of Stephen Ward.

The CCRC is empowered under Section 13(2)
of the 1995 Act to refer a conviction which has not
previously been subject to appeal if there is a 'real
possibility' that it would be overturned. There is no
requirement for an applicant to be the person
convicted, or a family member or personal representative – anyone may make an application for a CCRC
reference. There are circumstances where it will be

---

68   *R* v. *Hanratty* [2002] 2 Cr App R 30.

more appropriate, for example, where the applicant is the convicted defendant or someone with a
family or financial interest in his will, for the case to
be pursued by way of an 'out of time' appeal to the
Court of Appeal Criminal Division, without CCRC
involvement. In *Ward's* case this is not appropriate.
The court could only 'approve' an applicant on the
basis of a family relationship or a substantial financial or other interest (see 1968 Act, section 44A) and
although Stephen Ward had two brothers and twin
sisters, the relatives of a man whose waxwork soon
appeared in Madame Tussaud's chamber of horrors
have kept a low profile and may wish to remain
unidentified. Under the CCRC provisions in the 1995
Act, there is no need for an applicant: the commission may refer the case to the Court of Appeal of its
own volition, so long as there has been a 'conviction'
(see section 9(1)). Under section 9(2), once a case has
been referred it is treated as if the Court of Appeal
has already granted leave to appeal, which is why the
defendant is referred to in that court as an 'appellant'
rather than an applicant.

For these somewhat technical, but nonetheless
clear, reasons, I conclude that there is no need for a
relative or friend to be appointed to make an application to the CCRC. The communication to it of this

opinion by my solicitors, Messrs Simons Muirhead and Burton, should be sufficient to activate its statutory powers. The commission will, of course, be required to satisfy itself that there is a 'real possibility' of overturning the conviction, and that there are exceptional circumstances that justify a reference. I trust that, for the reasons I have given, both tests will be regarded as satisfied. The conviction of Stephen Ward stands as the worst unrequited miscarriage of justice in modern British history, and it is now time for it to be overturned.

NOTE ON SOURCES

There were a number of fairly 'instant' books on the *Ward* case, and more on the Profumo affair. The most authoritative is *The Trial of Stephen Ward* (Gollancz, 1964), by Ludovic Kennedy, a distinguished journalist and broadcaster whose books have made an important contribution to understanding how and why justice can miscarry. He attempted, subject to the acoustics in Court 1, to take down all the evidence at the trial, and much of the legal argument. I have used this book as the best 'unofficial transcript' (all references are to the 1965 Penguin edition) and have supplemented it with the various press reports published in Iain Crawford's book, *The Profumo Affair: A Crisis in Contemporary Society* (White Lodge Books, October 1963). This verifies most of Kennedy's transcription, and further confirmation is to be found in *Scandal '63 – A Study of the Profumo Affair* (Heinemann, 1963) by Clive Irving, Jeremy Wallington and Ron Hall. Wayland Young's instant insight *The Profumo Affair: Aspects of Conservatism* (Penguin Special, 1963) is a perceptive account of the political background. Lord Denning's report (September 1963) is readable but much less perceptive, even in the lavishly illustrated edition brought out in 2003 (Tim Coates, *Moments in History*). Denning was a brilliant civil lawyer who could write in tabloid prose, although he often misunderstood criminal law and could be a moral simpleton (he ruled once that a student could never make an acceptable career as a teacher because she had been found with a man in her room). Nonetheless his report is important in revealing dates and details of MI5 involvement, although it has been criticised for withholding or misrepresenting much of that organisation's contact with Ward, some of which was leaked to Nigel West for his book *A Matter of Trust: MI5, 1945–72* (Westintel, 1982) and appears in H. Montgomery Hyde, *A Tangled Web, Sex Scandals in British Politics and Society* (Futura, 1986). Further light is shed by the 'authorised' history of MI5 (*The Defence of the Realm*, by Christopher Andrew (Allen Lane, 2009)) which admits to meetings with Ward in 1962 and to the significant fact that he was used by the Foreign Office, with the approval of the Foreign Secretary, to pass information to the Soviets via Ivanov. The Foreign Office itself has never come clean about its use of Ward.

It was not until a quarter of a century had passed that the 'many witnesses of high estate and low' were prepared, even anonymously, to talk to journalists as reputable as Phillip Knightley and Caroline Kennedy. Their book, *An Affair of State: The Profumo Case and the Framing of Stephen Ward* (Jonathan Cape, 1987), was the first to pull the threads together and to discern a pattern of improper political direction and judicial manipulation. Much of the anger they rightfully arouse on behalf of the victim is alleviated by the amusement value of Richard Davenport-Hines's *An English Affair: Sex, Class, and Power in the Age of Profumo* (Collins, 2013). His sense of irony enlivens his contempt for the hypocrisy of the politicians, the humbug of the editors and the hubris of the judges. Other works that I have consulted include Pater Rawlinson QC's autobiography, *A Price Too High* (Weidenfeld & Nicolson, 1989), and 'Stephen Ward Speaks' (*Today* magazine, 1963), an instant paperback reproducing some private conversations with journalist Warwick Charleton and some critical reflection on the trial by judge Gerald Sparrow.

My thanks to Andrew Lloyd Webber for asking my opinion of Stephen Ward's trial. I have discussed the case with some who can still remember their involvement – Jeremy Hutchinson QC and Mandy Rice-Davies most helpfully – and mulled over the legal issues with Anthony Burton of Simons, Muirhead and Burton, and with my Doughty Street colleagues Richard Thomas and Toby Collis, and must thank Judy Rollinson, my PA, and Sam Carter at Biteback Publishing for arranging publication in record time. It was written as a pro-bono legal opinion for submission to the CCRC. I am grateful to Caroline Michel and Iain Dale for thinking that it merits publication. I have read Christopher Hampton's script for *Stephen Ward*, the new Lloyd Webber musical, which is remarkably faithful to the facts.

BRIEF CHRONOLOGY

1959

November	Ward meets Keeler at Murray's Club, Soho.

1960

March	Captain Eugene Ivanov arrives as Defence Attaché at Soviet embassy.

1961

January	Sir Colin Coote introduces Ward to Ivanov.
June	Count 1 period begins.
8 June	MI5 contacts Ward.
8/9 July	Cliveden weekend.
10/12 July	Ward reports to MI5.
August	Profumo dates Christine.

'Darling' letter on war office notepaper, to Christine from 'J'.

October   Ward and Keeler meet 'Lucky'
                   Gordon at *Rio* Café.

                   Keeler paid £50 by 'Charles'.

1962

February   Keeler leaves Wimpole Mews.

                   Foreign Office uses Ward to pass
                   information to Ivanov.

May   MI5 continues contact with Ward.

September   Count 2 period begins.

October   Mandy Rice-Davies moves to Wimpole
                   Mews after row with Rachman.

                   Mandy paid by Dr Savundra and has
                   sex (once) with Lord Astor.

29 November   Rachman dies after heart attack.

                   Mandy attempts suicide – parents
                   stay in Wimpole Mews.

14 December   Edgecombe shooting incident at
                   Wimpole Mews.

                   End of Count 2 period.

1963

January

26 January   Keeler tells Sgt Burrows that she
                   had sex with Profumo. Law officers

warned that Keeler may allege an affair with Profumo. He tells them that the association was innocent.

February

3 February   *News of the World* publishes picture of Keeler in a swimsuit. (Denning: 'Most people seeing that picture would realise what she was'.)

March

14 March   Edgecombe's trial. Keeler, the main witness, does not appear.

21 March   'Lunchtime O'Booze' insinuates the truth in *Private Eye*.
'The minister and the missing model' raised in Parliament by George Wigg, Richard Crossman and Barbara Castle.

22 March   Profumo meets five ministerial colleagues at 2 a.m.: law officers draft his 'personal statement'.
Later, makes personal statement in the House of Commons denying 'impropriety' with Keeler.

26 March   Ward meets George Wigg openly in Parliament tearoom.

27 March   Home Secretary (Sir Henry Brooke) 'feeling very suspicious towards

Ward'. (Denning) sends for head of MI5 (Hollis) and Commissioner of Metropolitan Police (Simpson), asks whether and how Ward can be prosecuted.

April

1 April   Investigation of Ward by Scotland Yard begins. Over next two months 140 potential witnesses are interviewed, Ward's telephone is tapped and his house and surgery watched.

18 April   Keeler is attacked by John Hamilton-Marshall but accuses 'Lucky' Gordon.

May

19 May   Ward complains to Home Secretary that he is being ruined by police investigation despite the fact that he has 'shielded' Profumo.

20 May   Home Secretary replies that police do not act under his direction. Ward copies his letter of 19 May to all newspaper editors, none of whom dare publish for fear of libel. Ward writes to Harold Wilson, declaring that Profumo had lied.

June

4 June	Profumo resigns.
5 June	'Lucky' Gordon tried for attacking Keeler. She swears that Gordon attacked her and that no witnesses were present. Police say they cannot find the two witnesses whom Gordon says were there and can confirm his innocence.
7 June	Gordon convicted, sentenced to three years in prison
8 June	Ward arrested. Denied bail.
9 June	Debate over Profumo affair in House of Commons. Ward described as a Soviet agent, Keeler and Rice-Davies as 'prostitutes' and 'harlots'.
28 June	Ward's committal proceedings: Keeler, Rice-Davies and Ricardo testify.

July

3 July	Ward committed for trial.
22 July	*R* v. *Ward* trial commences. Indictment on five counts: Count 1: Christine Keeler. Count 2: Marilyn Rice-Davies. Count 3: Ronna Ricardo and Vicki Barrett.

	Count 4: Procuring a woman (Sally Norie) for another.

Count 4: Procuring a woman (Sally Norie) for another.
Count 5: Procuring a woman (Miss R) for another.
Prosecution opening speech.
Keeler testifies.

23 July	Rice-Davies testifies.
24 July	Ricardo, Eynan, Barrett, Chief Inspector Herbert testify.
25/6 July	Ward testifies. Defence witnesses called to refute Barrett.
29 July	Noel Howard-Jones testifies. Defence counsel final speech. Prosecution final speech begins.
30 July	
9 a.m.	Court of Criminal Appeal: Jury verdict in *R* v. *Gordon* overturned. Chief Justice orders its decision to be hand-delivered to the Old Bailey.
10.30 a.m.	Old Bailey: Griffith-Jones concludes his final speech for prosecution, tells jury of Court of Appeal decision: 'It might be that Miss Keeler's evidence was completely truthful.' Judge begins summing-up and instructs jury that the fact that Ward

has been abandoned by his friends could mean it is less likely that he was telling the truth.

Late evening, Ward attempts suicide.

31 July   Judge refuses to adjourn trial. Completes summing-up and jury retires for four and a half hours, returns at 7.09 p.m. to acquit Ward on Counts 3–5, but to convict him on Counts 1 and 2.

August

3 August   Ward dies in hospital.

September

25 September   Lord Denning's Report Published. (Cmnd 2152)

October   Macmillan retires as Prime Minister.

December   Keeler pleads guilty to perjury at Gordon trial.

1964

January   Lord Chief Justice describes 'Lucky' Gordon trial as 'unfortunate'.

October   Labour wins election by four seats. Harold Wilson becomes Prime Minister.

APPENDIX A

STATEMENT BY SIR DAVID TUDOR-PRICE

Sir David was junior counsel for Stephen Ward. He subsequently became a Senior Treasury Counsel at the Old Bailey (like Griffith-Jones before him) and then a High Court judge. He made this statement, for publication, to author Caroline Kennedy, shortly before his death, about the way Lord Chief Justice Parker manipulated the decision in the Gordon appeal so that it would undermine, rather than assist, Ward's defence.

This was a matter that still rankles with me. It has left a burning sense of injustice. The only possible purpose of the Lord Chief Justice's action was to cut away the foundations of what James Burge had been saying to the Ward jury. The Court of Criminal Appeal said that it thought that Gordon's conviction was unsatisfactory, but it was not saying that

Christine Keeler was a perjurer. Words to that effect were read out by Archie Marshall to the Ward jury in his summing-up, for the very purpose of discrediting, or rather taking away, the value of the point made by James Burge, and that's something I've never known done before or since. The Ward case was easily the most celebrated case in my whole career. I suppose I was young and impressionable, but I was left with an unpleasant taste in the mouth; that this really had not been just… There must have been great pressure for a conviction. The 'Lucky' Gordon appeal coinciding with Ward's trial and coming to the conclusion it did was totally reprehensible.

Quoted in Knightley and Kennedy, *An Affair of State: The Profumo Case and the Framing of Stephen Ward* (Cape, 1987), p. 239 and p. 254.

APPENDIX B

LORD GOODMAN'S OPINION

Lord Goodman's Verdict

Arnold Goodman was a renowned solicitor at the time, and later Master of University College, Oxford. He followed the Ward trial closely to advise Penguin books on whether they could publish Ludovic Kennedy's The Trial of Stephen Ward, *which had been threatened with proceedings for contempt of court.*

It will be remembered that Stephen Ward was picked on as a victim to pacify the Establishment in the unhappy Profumo affair. There had to be someone upon whom they could take out their sense of indignation and Stephen Ward was outrageously prosecuted for living on the earnings of prostitutes. A prostitute is, of course, a street-walker, and however indulgent the morals of Miss Keeler and the other ladies involved, they were not by any stretch of imagination streetwalkers. Nor, on a fair assessment of the situation, which after a careful study of the book and long discussions with Ludovic Kennedy I can claim to have made, did Stephen Ward live on their earnings. His household was raffish, Bohemian, and the young ladies came and went, partially as guests, partially as tenants, occasionally contributing to a common household fund. However, all of this could be presented, if the legal machine was set in motion, in the most unfavourable of lights. I do not know of any prosecution more outrageous than this one or where there was a more deliberate and wicked attempt to victimise the accused. In many ways Ward was not a particularly worthy individual, but on that score who would 'scape whipping?

Arnold Goodman, 'Tell them, I'm On My Way' (Chapmans, 1993), p. 174.

APPENDIX C

BERNARD LEVIN ON WARD'S TRIAL

Bernard Levin was for many years the best-informed and most acerbic critic of England's laws and lawyers. In 1963 he was a regular commentator on That Was The Week That Was. *He wrote this at the end of the decade for an acclaimed book about the swinging 'pendulum years' of the 1960s.*

Of the trial of Stephen Ward the only thing that can now be said with any certainty is that he was not guilty as charged, and that apart from the judge and, presumably, the prosecuting counsel, – that same Mervyn Griffith-Jones whose concern for the morals of other people's wives and servants played so notable a part in another celebrated trial of the 1960s – few could seriously have believed that he was. What he was much more widely believed to be was what prosecuting counsel called him: 'a thoroughly filthy fellow';

and the phrase (which seemed to come most naturally from Mr Griffith-Jones's disdainful mouth, and can be marked down to him for such credit as is fitting, along with his subsequent definition in the same case of a respectable girl as one who doesn't want to go to bed with anyone) may stand as the epitaph on at any rate one side of Ward's gravestone, the one carved there by the disapproval of society.

The conduct of the case, the obvious inadequacy, to put it inadequately, of by far the greater part of the prosecution's evidence, the zeal with which Mr Griffith-Jones hunted his prey – these and other aspects of a miserable miscarriage of justice may stand as a monument to an episode of which the British legal system has no reason to be proud, and may even, if such a feeling can ever penetrate the self-protection in which the practitioners of that system are wrapped (the judge did not fail to say at one point: 'We of the Bar are men of the world'), be by now ashamed. Yet one single episode of the case must be recounted again, for it epitomises those aspects of it that, with the 1960s left behind, now seem almost unbelievable, so impossible is it that they could occur, at any rate in the same form, today. It is impossible, for instance, that evidence as *obviously* perjured as was much of that given by most of the girls in the case could be treated

seriously now, if only because in the different atmosphere now prevailing a rather more sophisticated
approach to prosecution witnesses would be almost
bound to exist on the part of the jury, and even police
evidence is often now treated in a rather more robust
way than was apparently the case at the time.

The moment at which the lost atmosphere of the
1960s – the years in which things could happen that
could not happen now – was shown at its clearest was
during the last day but one of the trial. Not far away,
while the Ward trial was proceeding at the Old Bailey,
the Court of Criminal Appeal was hearing submis-
sions on behalf of Aloysius Gordon. He was one of the
men with whom Christine Keeler had been involved,
and whose success with her had resulted in the affray
between him and John Edgecombe, and ultimately
in the Sarajevo-like shots which Edgecombe fired.
Gordon had been charged with assaulting her; he was
found guilty, and sentenced to three years' imprisonment. But after his conviction enquiries had continued,
the strands in the Profumo affair and the Ward case
having become entangled with others not strictly
relevant to them, and as a result of these enquiries
Gordon's appeal was allowed, on the grounds that,
had the new information, together with the witnesses
who could have supported it, been available at his

trial, it would not have been right to convict him. The statements that the Court of Criminal Appeal had before it were such as to cast reasonable doubt, to put it mildly (which is the way the court was careful to put it), on the evidence given by Christine Keeler at Gordon's trial. (In fact, she was subsequently charged with perjury and sentenced to nine months' imprisonment, though it was doubtless thought by those who decide such things that it would have verged upon bad taste to engage Mr Mervyn Griffith-Jones to lead for the prosecution.)

Now it is inconceivable that the Court of Criminal Appeal, which on this occasion was sitting under the Lord Chief Justice, did not know that while they were quashing Gordon's conviction the trial of Stephen Ward, which depended to at least as great an extent as that of Gordon on the evidence of Miss Keeler, was proceeding. And before the Ward trial had proceeded for many more hours what had been said in the appeal court was known at the Old Bailey and indeed referred to by Mr Griffith-Jones in his closing speech, when he blandly dismissed it as irrelevant, on the grounds that the appeal judges had not ruled that Christine Keeler's evidence in the Gordon case was perjured, only that the absence of the witnesses who would have sworn that it *was* perjured provided the 'reasonable doubt' the existence of which in a jury's mind must prevent conviction.

Many arguments have been deployed over this matter, and the law was subsequently amended to enable the Court of Criminal Appeal to order a fresh trial in such cases. The conduct of the appeal judges has been defended on the grounds that they were unable to produce (because no evidence is given in an appeal court, only arguments on law) the statements they had before them, which cast not merely reasonable but overwhelming doubt on Christine Keeler's veracity. The defence is absurd: nothing inhibited the Court of Criminal Appeal from saying whatever they wished on the subject, from quoting the statements directly or in their own paraphrase, or indeed from simply making known the dangers of relying on Christine Keeler's evidence. Nothing can stop a judge from saying what he wants to, least of all Lord Parker, who is not noticeably reticent, let alone taciturn, when it comes to expressing his views. Moreover, knowing as they did what was happening at the Old Bailey, it was their clear *duty* to make the strongest possible indication of the reasonable doubts now surrounding Christine Keeler as a witness, for the appalling truth is that not only had she been lying in the Gordon case, as her subsequent trial for perjury established, *but she had repeated some of the very same lies in her evidence against Ward*. Nobody has ever explained why the judge in the Ward trial did not immediately adjourn it, when he heard the news from the Court of Criminal Appeal, until this crucial matter could be cleared up one way or the other, for to shelter behind the appeal court's statement that their own decision did not establish that Christine Keeler had been lying, only that a reasonable doubt now entered where it had not been before, is clearly inadequate; a reasonable doubt in one court is a reasonable doubt in another, especially when it refers not only to the same witness but to the same evidence. Shortly afterwards those reasonable doubts were brought into the light, at Miss Keeler's own trial, and there seen to be very reasonable indeed, so reasonable, in fact, that she was sent to prison on the strength of them. But by that time Ward had been convicted and was dead by his own hand, and Mr Griffith-Jones was a year closer to the judgeship to which he was appointed in 1967. (There was perhaps some tiny element of consolation in the fact that so fastidious a man should have become the Common Sergeant.)

At the end of the trial a distinguished and well-known High Court judge remarked privately, after reading the reports of the case, that, had it been tried before him, he would never have allowed it to go to the jury, and would have had some pertinent observations to make about the bringing of it. And that, presumably, will have to stand as the epitaph on the other side of Stephen Ward's tombstone.

Bernard Levin, *The Pendulum Years: Britain and the Sixties* (Pan Books, 1972), pp. 82–5.

APPENDIX D

QUESTIONS IN THE HOUSE OF LORDS, 18 JULY 2013

'To ask Her Majesty's Government whether they intend to release the records and files of the 1963 inquiry which led to the publication of Lord Denning's report The Circumstances Leading to the Resignation of the Former Secretary of State for War, Mr J. D. Profumo.'

Lord Wallace of Saltaire: My Lords, no decision has yet been taken on the future of the information held by the Cabinet Office on the Denning inquiry.

Lord Lexden: Does my noble friend agree that the records relating to Lord Denning's inquiry constitute an immensely valuable historical source which, if released, would deepen our knowledge and understanding of one of the most sensational political scandals in British history? Does he also agree that a cloud of suspicion hangs over the Denning report? It has been described as 'the raciest and most readable blue book ever published'. It has also been depicted as an endorsement of tainted evidence from journalists and the police used at the trial of one of the principal protagonists in the extraordinary drama, Dr Stephen Ward. That is the view of Mr Richard Davenport-Hines, author of the latest detailed account of the Profumo affair. There was collusion between the police and journalists fifty years ago on a scale that would make Lord Justice Leveson's hair stand on end. Do we not need to see if we can get to the truth through the release of the Denning records?

Lord Wallace of Saltaire: My Lords, I thank the noble Lord for giving me the opportunity to go into this fascinating case. There has been a series of constructive non-decisions. Had decisions been taken on several occasions, the papers would have been destroyed. Indeed, in a debate in this House in April 1977, Lord Denning announced that the papers had been destroyed. The following day the Lord Chancellor stood up to say that he had not permitted this and that this action had not been taken. Given, however, the assurances Lord Denning gave to all of those he interviewed that these records were entirely confidential and that they would never be published, it seems acceptable that they should not be published while those who were interviewed by Lord Denning are still alive.

Lord Tyler: My Lords, given the suspicions at the time of Soviet espionage and all the excitement of Cabinet members being involved in regular orgies, it is perhaps not surprising that fifty years on we still do not know the truth of the Profumo affair. Will my noble friend tell us by what criteria it is decided how much time has to lapse before such matters are made public? Who takes that decision? When and how are those decisions reviewed and by whom – or are these matters also secret?

Lord Wallace of Saltaire: My Lords, I am conscious that there are several Members of this House who would love to write the next book on the Profumo affair. If I were asked to advise on the decision on this, I would say that we should hold to the principle not that the content should never be published but that it should not be published while those who gave confidential information on the assurance that it would not be published are still alive – and some of those who gave that evidence are still alive. The decision will have to be approved by the Lord Chancellor and the Minister for the Cabinet Office. The Master of the Rolls – as Lord Denning was then – also plays a role in such decisions as chair of the advisory board on public records.

Lord Armstrong of Ilminster: My Lords, I declare an interest as one who formerly had the custodianship of these papers. I can confirm that the evidence was taken by Lord Denning on the specific understanding that it would never be published. I think that one would need to be very bold to go back on that, certainly while people who gave evidence to the Denning inquiry or who were involved in events are still alive, and perhaps during the lifetime of their descendants.

Does the Minister agree that it will need something like 100 years before one can consider whether these papers should be published?

Lord Wallace of Saltaire: My Lords, I do not wish to take a decision on that, either.

Lord Stevenson of Balmacara: My Lords, we are in an era where freedom of information and changes to the way in which information circulates mean that many decisions need serious review. Can the Minister confirm that this is a one-off situation? Or is he articulating a new policy whereby inquiries of the type led by Lord Denning will give rise to the curious situation of papers not being held in the Public Record Office in the way that all other papers are held?

Lord Wallace of Saltaire: I can give an assurance that this was a very exceptional circumstance. Officials have looked back at the archive on a number of occasions and have assured others, including myself, that there are still some sensational personal items in here which would be embarrassing if released. Therefore this is very much an exceptional case. The promises given by Lord Denning to those he interviewed were also rather exceptional. Therefore the line which the Government are in effect taking is correct; that is, to not decide at present either to destroy or to release the papers but to review the situation from time to time in the light of how many of those who gave evidence are still with us.

Lord Lloyd Webber: My Lords, I declare an interest in that my new musical is about Stephen Ward and I am presenting a documentary on him for ITV. Is the Minister aware – this is what concerns me – that the fact that these files will be closed for a staggering eighty-three years gives rise to an awful lot of unhealthy speculation about who the individuals might be within the files?

Lord Wallace of Saltaire: My Lords, we have not yet decided whether they will remain closed for eighty-three years. It is fairly clear who all the individuals in the files are: they are those who were interviewed by Lord Denning.

Lord Richard: My Lords, I confess that I am slightly baffled by this. Did Lord Denning have the authority to give those assurances? I thought that the release of public documents was governed by various rules and regulations – there may even be an Act – that there was a thirty-year rule and a fifty-year rule, and that that was, so to speak, part of the governmental fabric. Is the chairman of an inquiry that has been set up by the government in those circumstances to inquire into a matter like this entitled to give an assurance which, in effect, eats into or may even destroy the purposes of the various rules and regulations about release?

Lord Wallace of Saltaire: My Lords, this decision has been reviewed several times. As I remarked, the review has considered whether the files should be destroyed, maintained or released. As the noble Lord is well aware, there are a number of cases, particularly those with security and defence issues, where papers are retained for more than fifty, thirty or twenty years. That has to have the approval of what is called a Lord Chancellor's Instrument. It would now be appropriate to consider whether a formal Lord Chancellor's Instrument needs to be applied to these files. I will add that at the time, Lord Denning refused to allow the head of the security services access to the papers.